Authentic GUITAR-TAB Edition
Includes Complete Solos™

MW00814166

JETHRO TULL

GUITAR ANTHOLOGY SERIES

CONTENTS

Transcribed by KENN CHIPKIN and DANNY BEGELMAN

Project Manager: COLGAN BRYAN
Project Coordinator: SHERYL ROSE
Book Design: JOSEPH KLUCAR
Art Layout: MICHAEL RAMSAY

Cover Art

Stand Up
© 1969 Chrysalis Records

Benefit (Released 1970)
© 1970 Chrysalis Records

Aqualung
© 1971 Chrysalis Records

Thick as a Brick
© 1972 Chrysalis Records

Living in the Past
© 1972 Chrysalis Records

WarChild
© 1974 Chrysalis Records

Minstrel in the Gallery
© 1975 Chrysalis Records

Too Old to Rock 'n' Roll: Too Young to Die!
© 1976 Chrysalis Records

AQUALUNG

Words and Music by
IAN ANDERSON and
JENNIE ANDERSON

Gtr. 2 Capo 3rd fret:

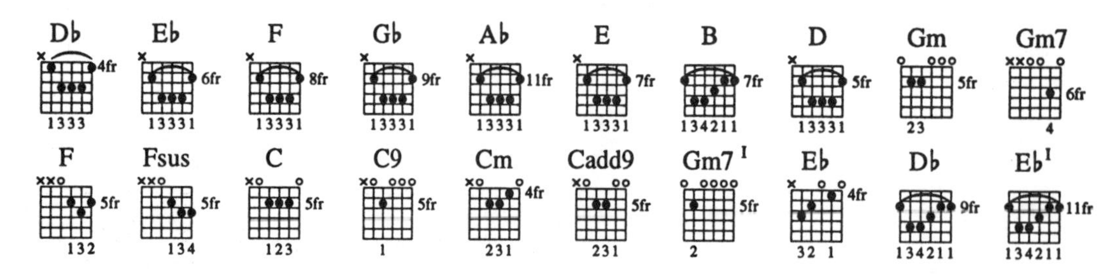

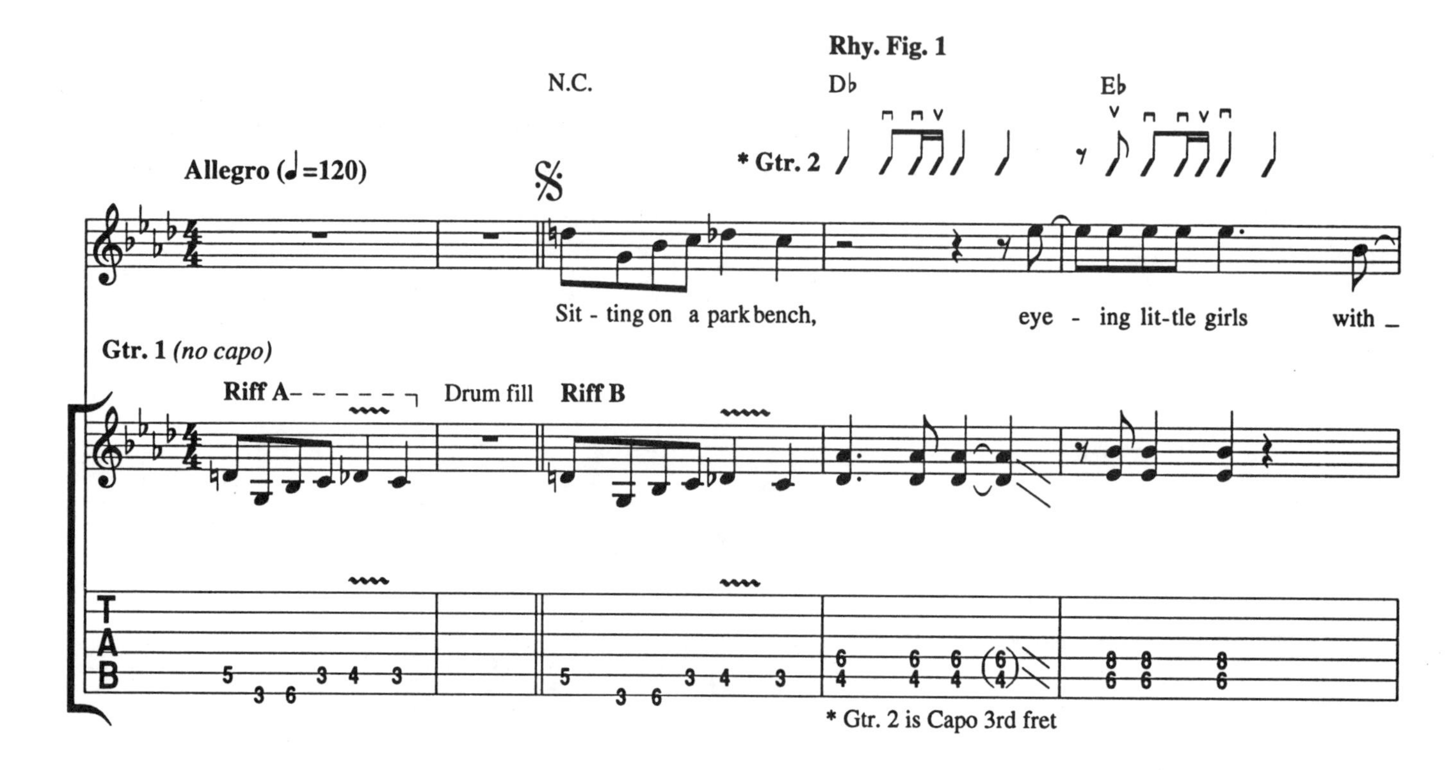

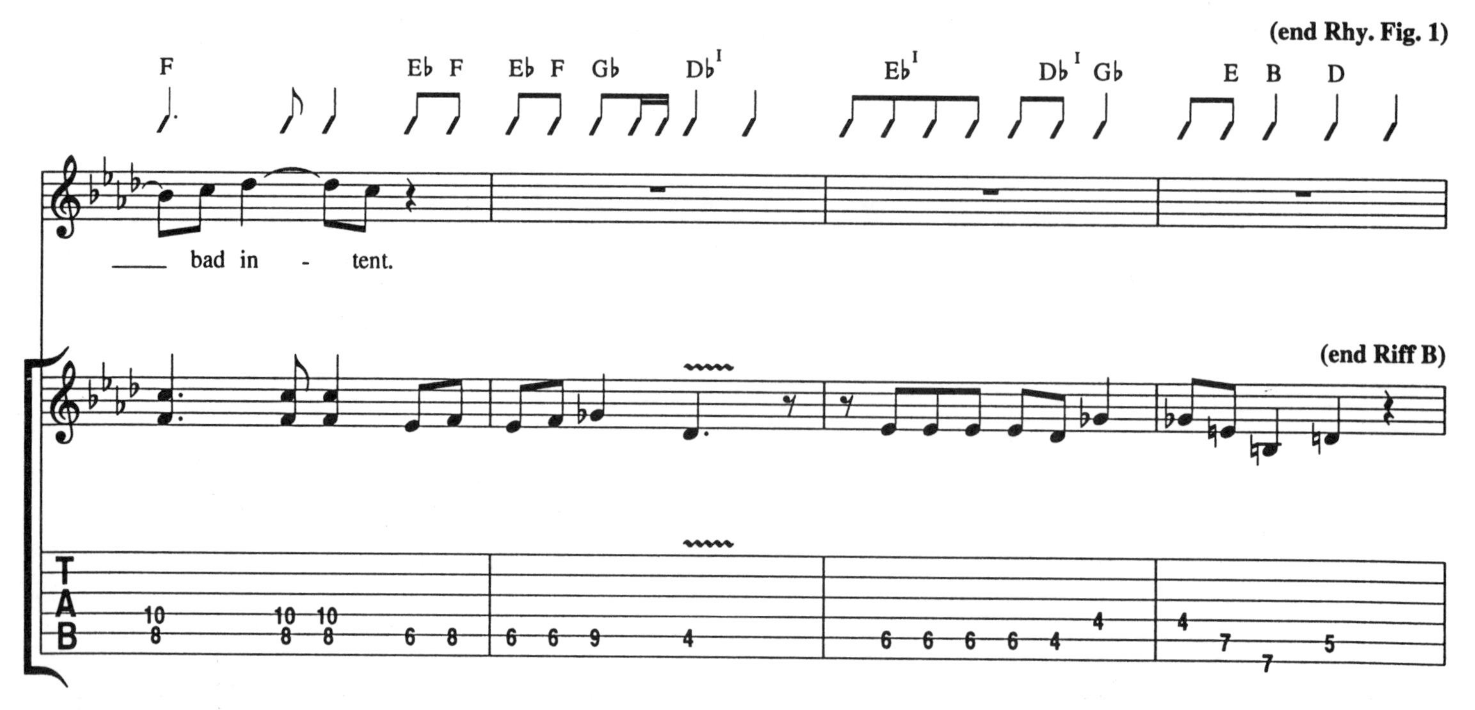

w/Riff B
w/Rhy. Fig. 1
N.C.
Db
Eb
F
Eb F
Snot's run-ning down his nose,
greas - y fin - gers smear - ing shab-by clothes,
Eb F Gb Db I
Eb I
Db I Gb
E B D
w/Riff B
hey Aq - ua - lung.
Dry-ing in the cold sun,
w/Rhy. Fig. 1 & Riff B
watch - ing as the fril - ly pant - ies run,
Riff C
T
A
B
hey Aq - ua - lung.
(end Riff C)
w/Riff B
w/Riff C & Rhy. Fig. 1
Feel - ing like a dead duck,
spit - ting out piec - es of his
bro - ken luck,
E I
oh Aq - ua - lung.
(2nd time) hey

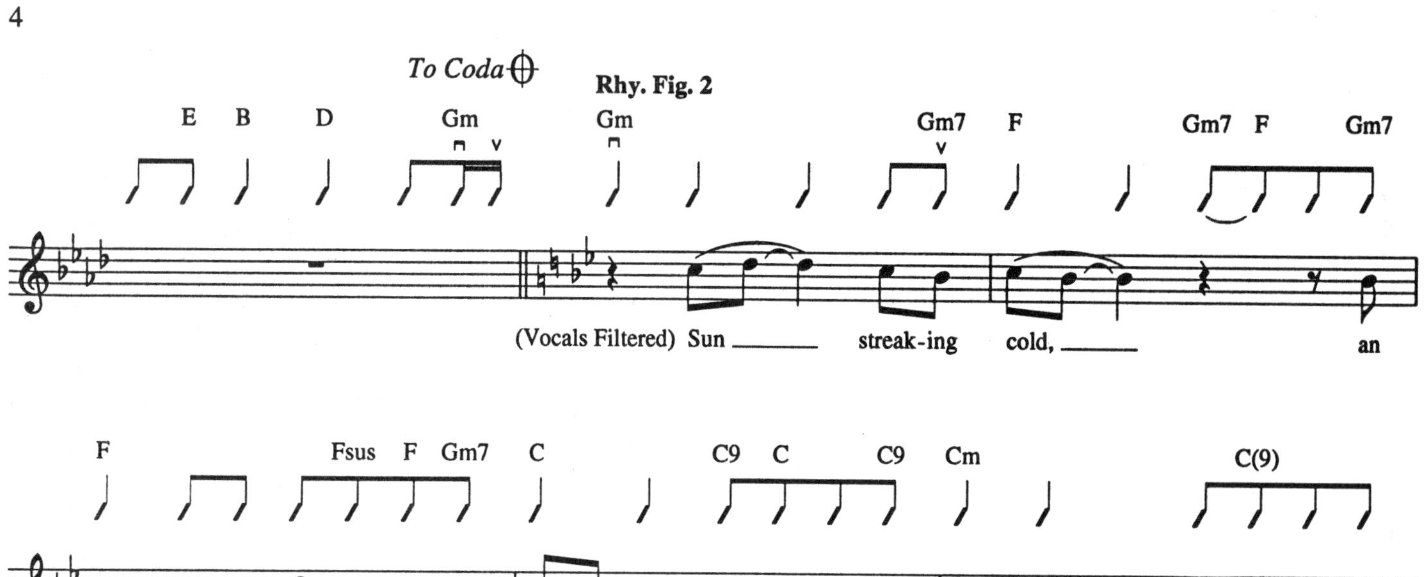

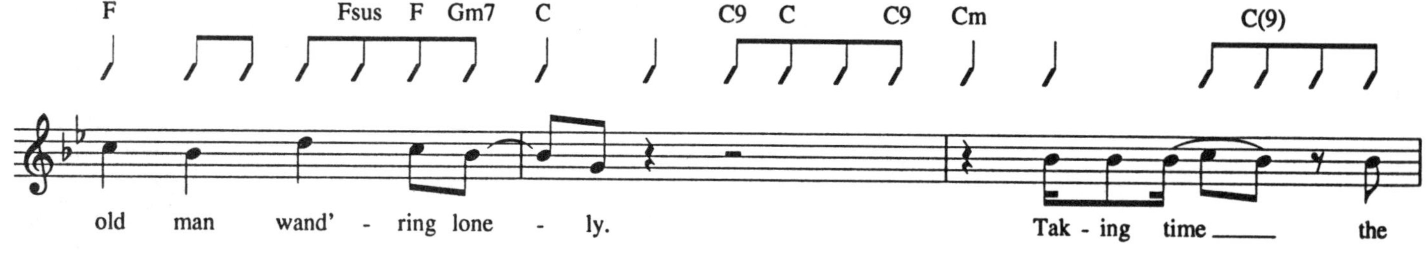

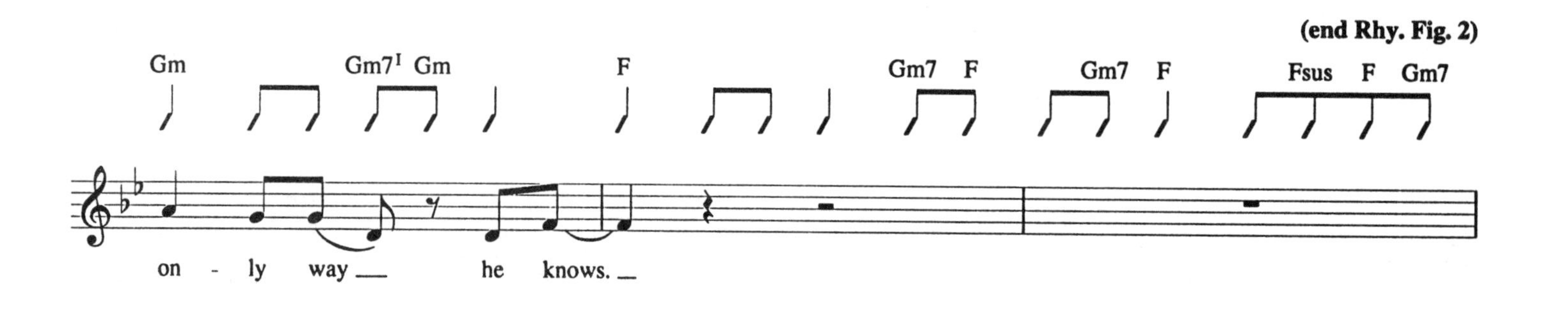

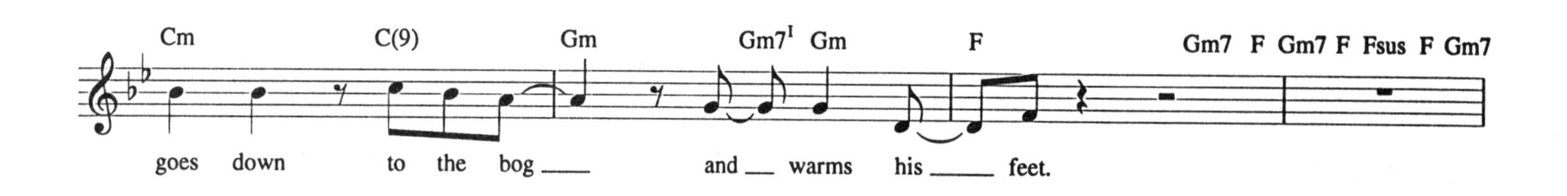

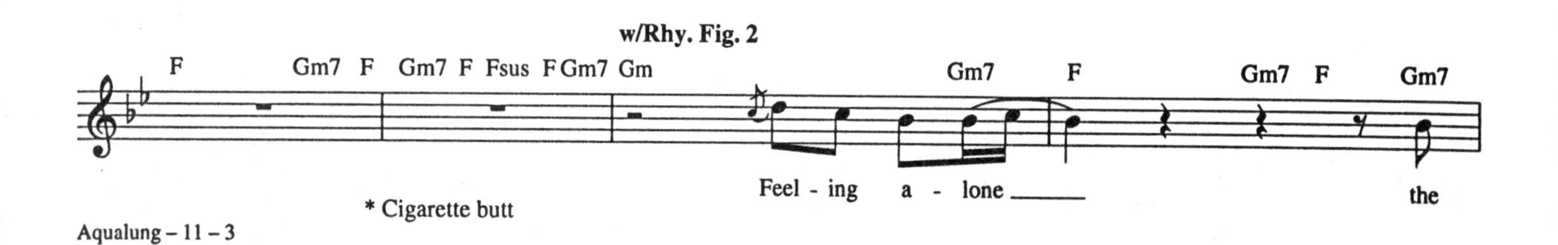

* Cigarette butt

F Fsus F Gm7 C C9 C C9 Cm C(9) Gm Gm7I Gm
ar - my's up the road sal - va - tion a la mode and a cup of
w/Rhy. Fig. 2
F Gm7 F F Gm7 F Fsus F Gm7 Gm Gm7 F Gm7 F Gm7
tea. Aqu - a - lung my friend don't you
F Fsus F Gm7 C C9 C C9 Cm C(9)
start a - way un - eas - y. You poor old sod you
Rhy. Fig. 3
Gm Gm7I Gm F Gm7 F Gm7 F Fsus F Gm7 F Gm7 F
see it's on - ly me.
♩=176 Presto
F Gm7 F Fsus F Gm7 Gm F Gm7
Do you still re - mem - ber De -
F Gm Gm7I Gm
cem - ber's fog - gy freeze, when the ice that clings on
F Gm7 F Gm Gm7I
to your beard was scream - ing ag - o - ny? (sans filter:) Hey! Then you

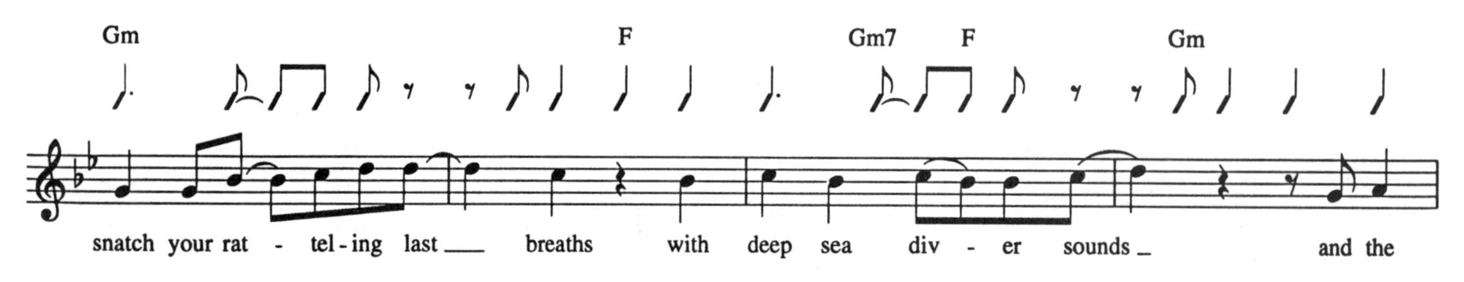
Gm F Gm7 F Gm
snatch your rat - tel - ing last breaths with deep sea div - er sounds and the

Cm F Gm7 F Fsus F Gm7
flow-ers bloom like mad - ness in the spring.

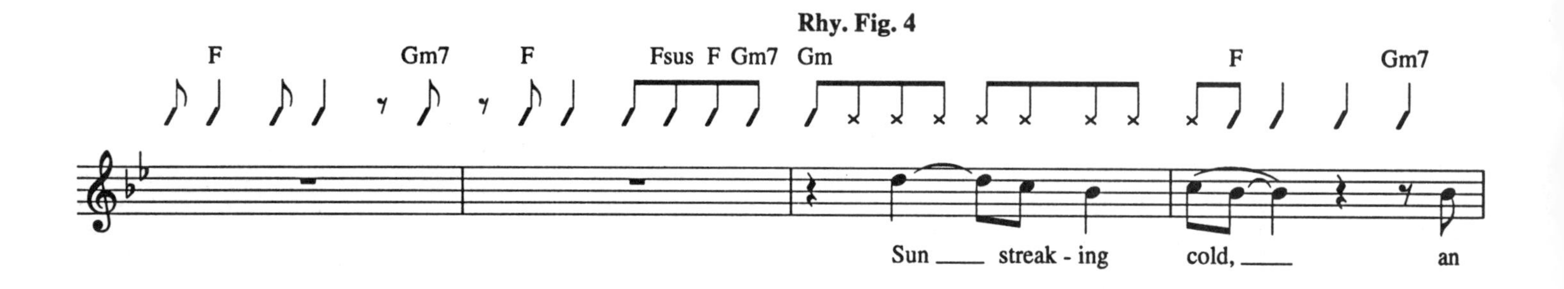
Rhy. Fig. 4
F Gm7 F Fsus F Gm7 Gm F Gm7
Sun streak - ing cold, an

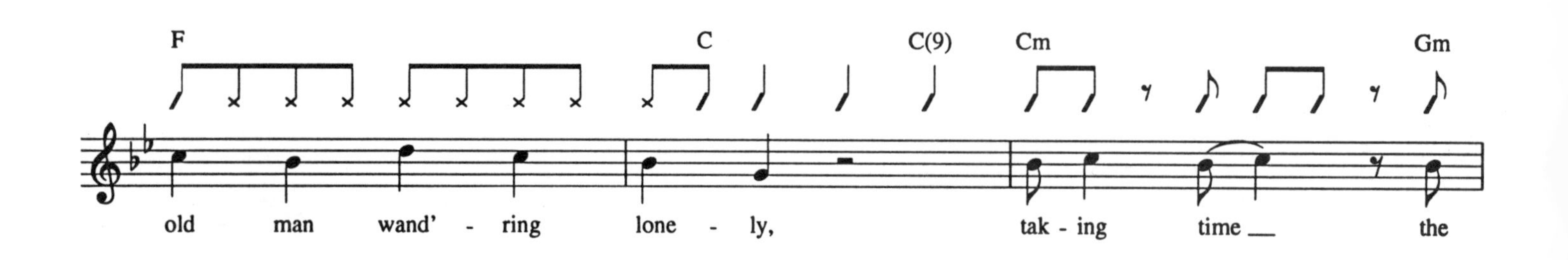
F C C(9) Cm Gm
old man wand' - ring lone - ly, tak - ing time the

Gm Gm7 F Gm7 F Fsus F Gm7
on - ly way he knows.

w/Rhy. Fig. 4
Gm F Gm7 F C C(9)
Leg hurt - ing bad, as he bends to pick a dog - end, he

Cm Gm Gm7 F Gm7 F Fsus F Gm7
goes down to the bog and warms his feet.

F Gm7 F Fsus F Gm7 Gm F Gm7
w/Rhy. Fig. 4
Wo - o - ho ho. Feel - ing a - lone, the

F C C(9) Cm Gm
ar - my's up the road, sal - va - tion a la mode.

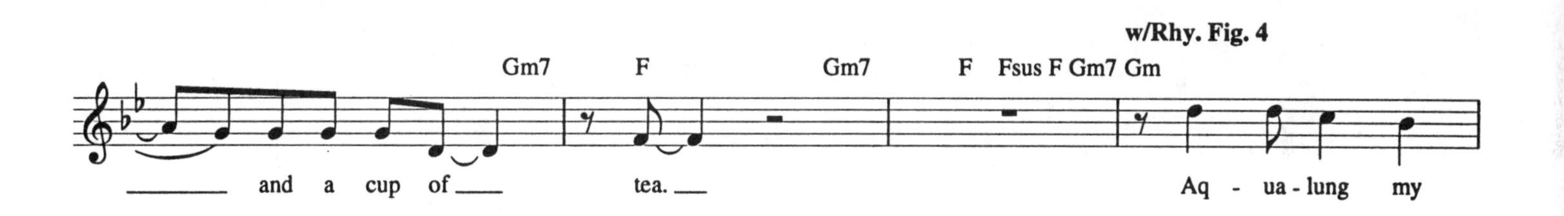
Gm7 F Gm7 F Fsus F Gm7 Gm
w/Rhy. Fig. 4
and a cup of tea. Aq - ua - lung my

F Gm7 F C C(9) Cm Gm
friend, don't you start a - way un - eas - y. You poor old sod, you

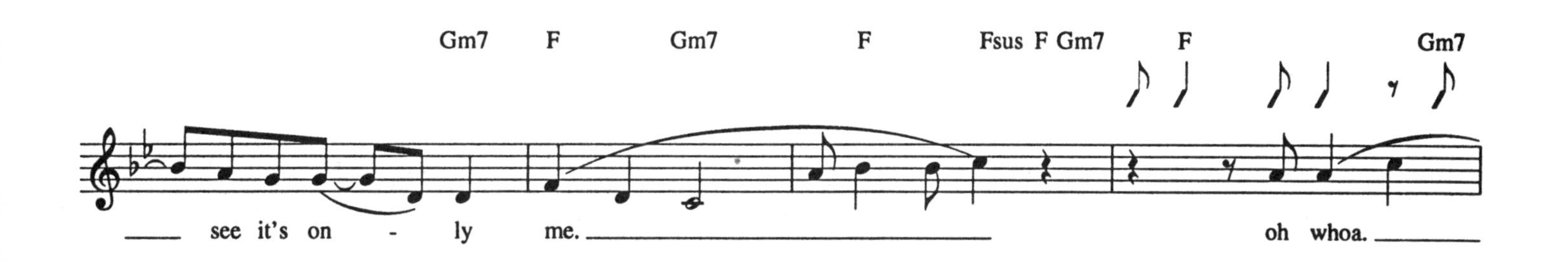
Gm7 F Gm7 F Fsus F Gm7 F Gm7
see it's on - ly me. oh whoa.

Interlude:
F
Gm
F
Gtr. 1
T
A
B
6 8 10 (10)
(10)
3 2 3 2 3 (3)
C
(Doubled by 2nd guitar)
Cm
Gm
Feedback (2nd gtr.)
Feedback (1st gtr.)
8va
pp
f

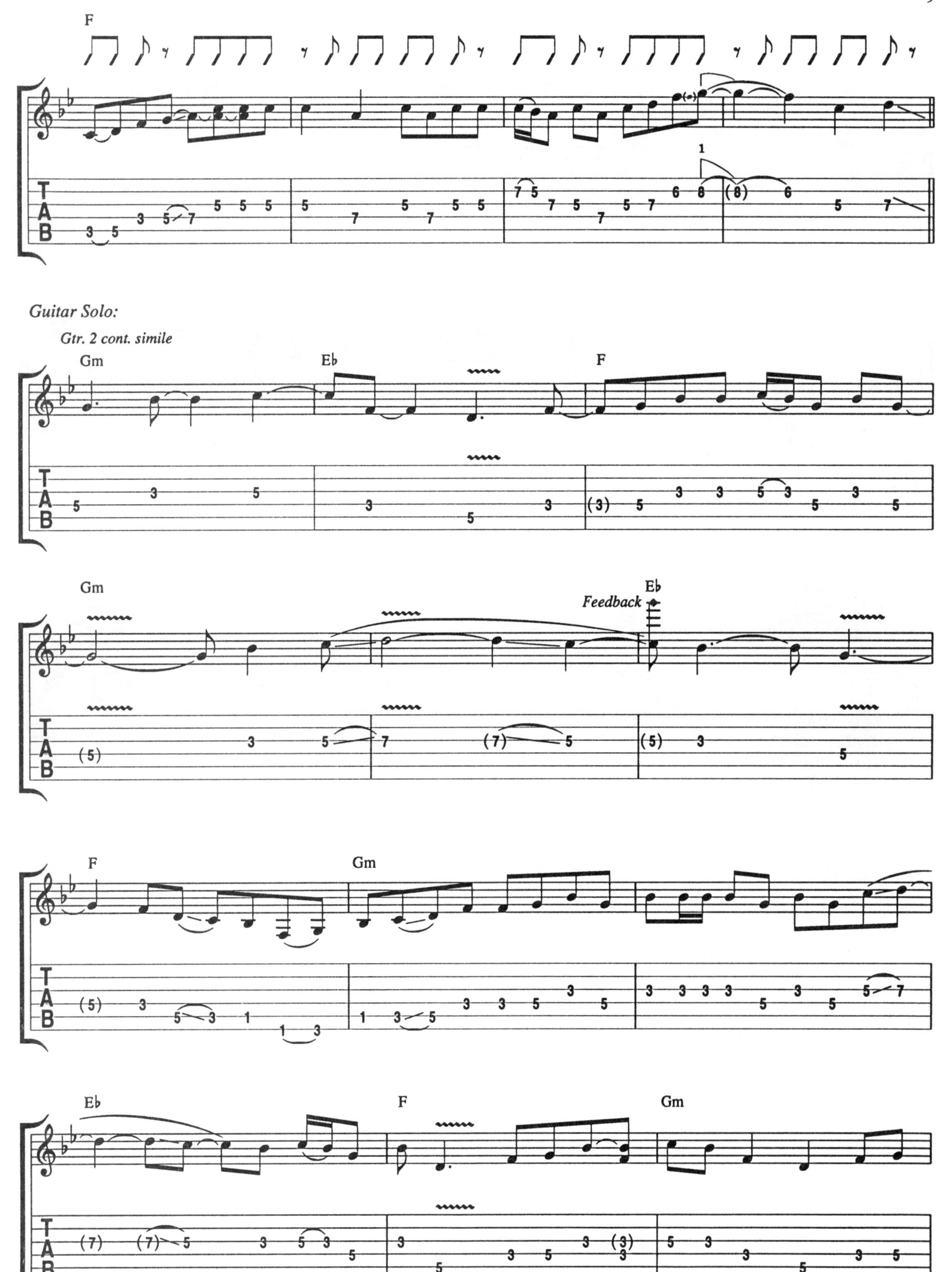
F
Guitar Solo:
Gtr. 2 cont. simile
Gm
Eb
F
Gm
Feedback
Eb
F
Gm
Eb
F
Gm

E♭
F
Gm
E♭
III pos.
F
Gm
E♭
F
Gm
E♭
F
C VI 1/3
Gm

Eb
F
(10)
(8)
Allegro (♩=120)
w/Rhy. Fig. 2
Gm
Gm7
F
Fsus
Dee dee dee dee, dee dee dee dee dee dee,
C
C9
Cm
C(9)
(Gm7I)
dee dee dee dee dee dee dee dee dee dee.
w/Rhy. Fig. 2
Aqu - a - lung my
friend, don't you s - start a - way un - eas - y. You

w/Riff D (Gtr. 2)
Cm
Gm
F
Gm7 F
poor old sod, you see it's on - ly me, yeah.
F Gm7 F
Fsus F Gm7
F
Gm7 F
Gm7 F Gm7 F
Hmm.
Acoustic Tacet
w/Riff A
w/Riff A
(Drum fill)
D.S. 𝄋 al Coda
Coda
Acoustic Tacet
w/Riff A
(Drum fill)
w/Riff A
(Drum fill)
w/Riff A
Acoustic and Electric guitar:
♩=86
D♭
Oh oh
E♭
F
oh, Aq - ua - lung.
Riff D
Gtr. 2
Cm
Gm
T
A
B

BOURÉE

Words and Music by
IAN ANDERSON

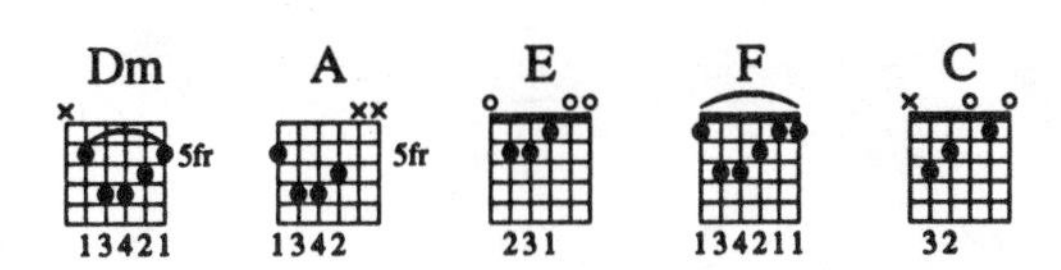

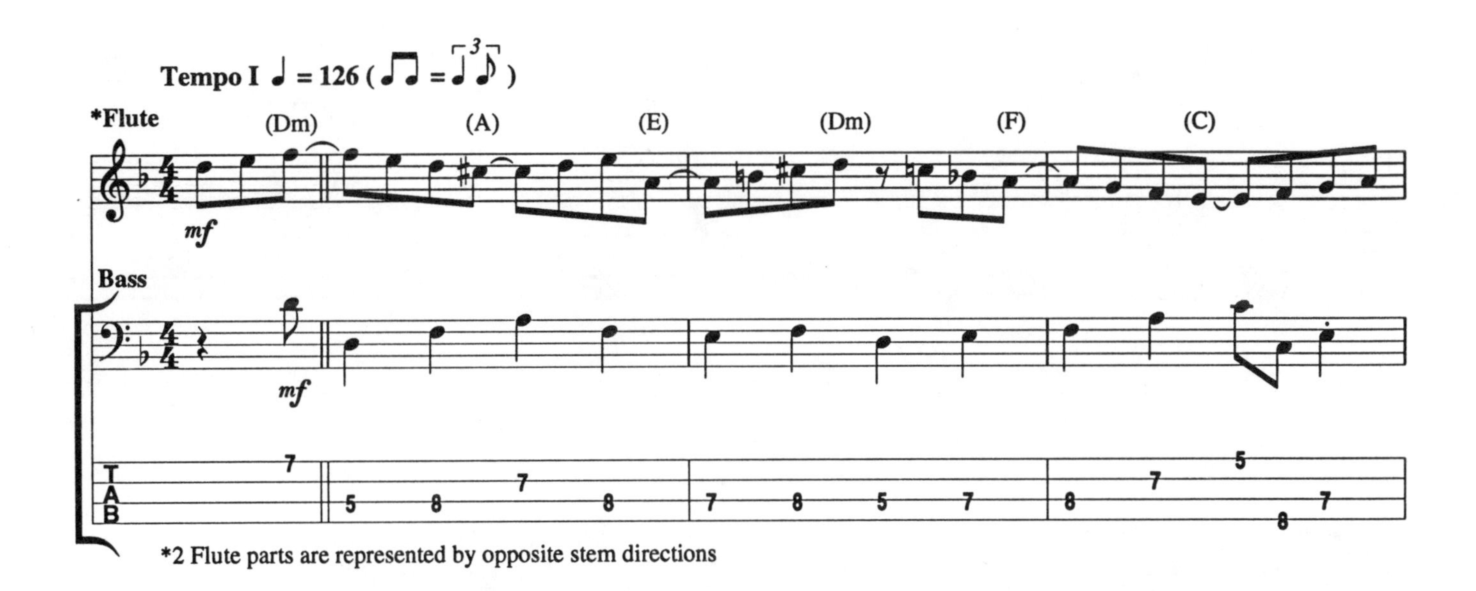

*2 Flute parts are represented by opposite stem directions

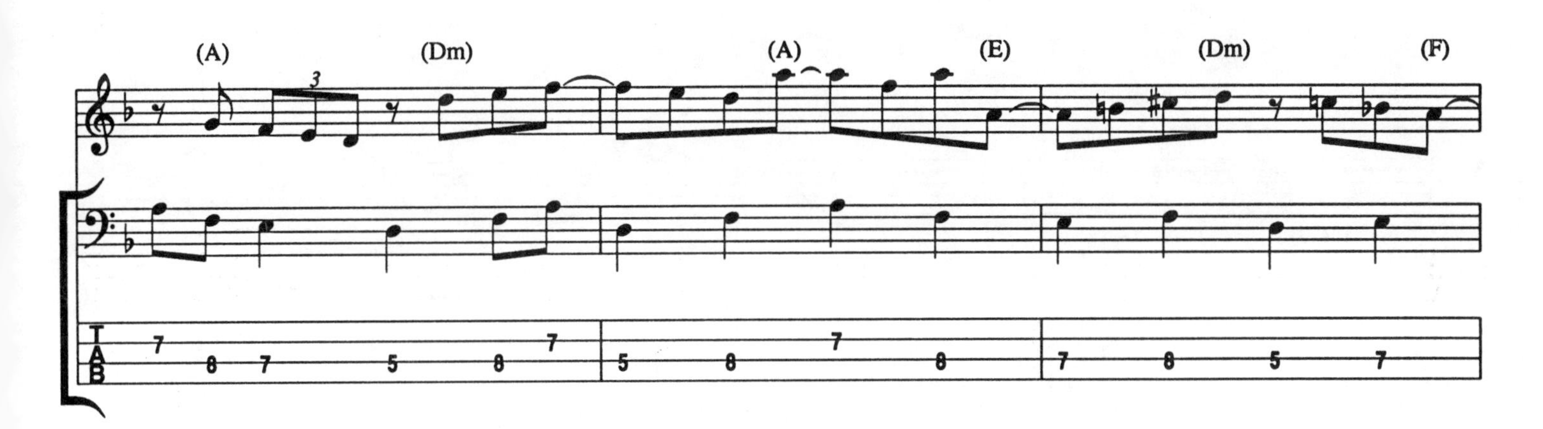

Dm
F
C
A
Dm
3
3
3
A
E
Dm
F
Flute Solo I: (ad lib.)
Dm
A
E
Dm
F
C
A
Dm
3
3

A
E
Dm
F
C
F
Dm
A
C
Dm
C
Dm
A
Dm
A
C
Dm
C
Dm
A
Dm
Flute Break: (ad lib.)
Dm

Gtr. 1
Flute Solo II: (ad lib.)
Dm7
Gm7
Bass
Dm7
Gm7
Dm
A
C
Dm
C
Dm
A
Dm

Bass Solo: (ad lib.)
Dm
A
E
Dm
F
C
A
Dm
(Cont. rhy. simile)
A
E
Dm
F
C
F
N.C. (Solo continues)
7
rit.
Flute
C5
Dm
(C)
(F/C)
(C/G)
Dm
a tempo
(Dm)
(A)
(E)
(Dm)
(F)
(C)
(A)
(Dm)
(A)
(E)

(Dm)
(F)
Dm
A
E
Dm
F
C
(Cont. rhy. simile)
A
Dm
A
E
Dm
F
C
F
Dm
A
T
A
B

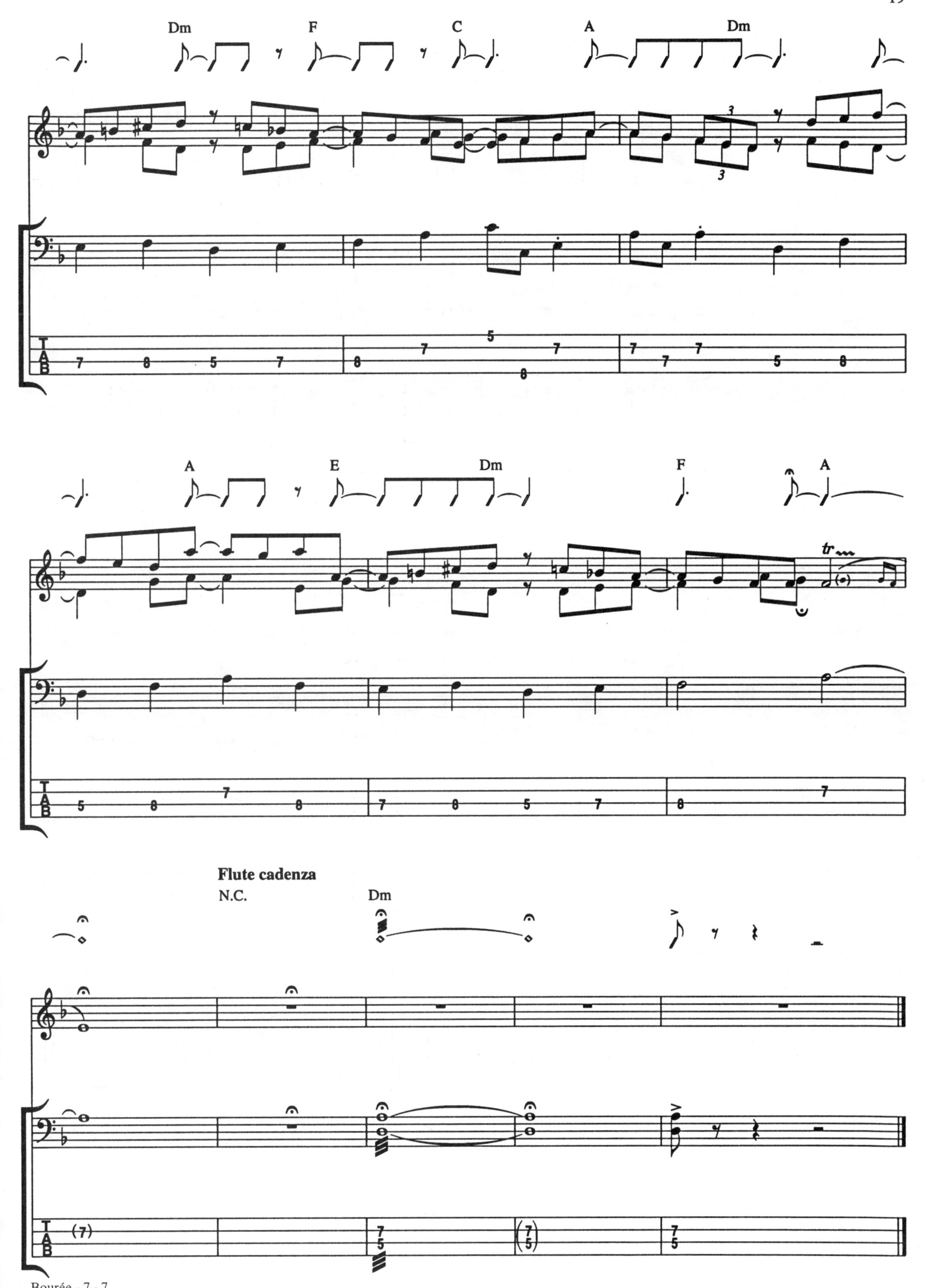
Dm
F
C
A
Dm
A
E
Dm
F
A
tr
Flute cadenza
N.C.
Dm

BUNGLE IN THE JUNGLE

Words and Music by
IAN ANDERSON

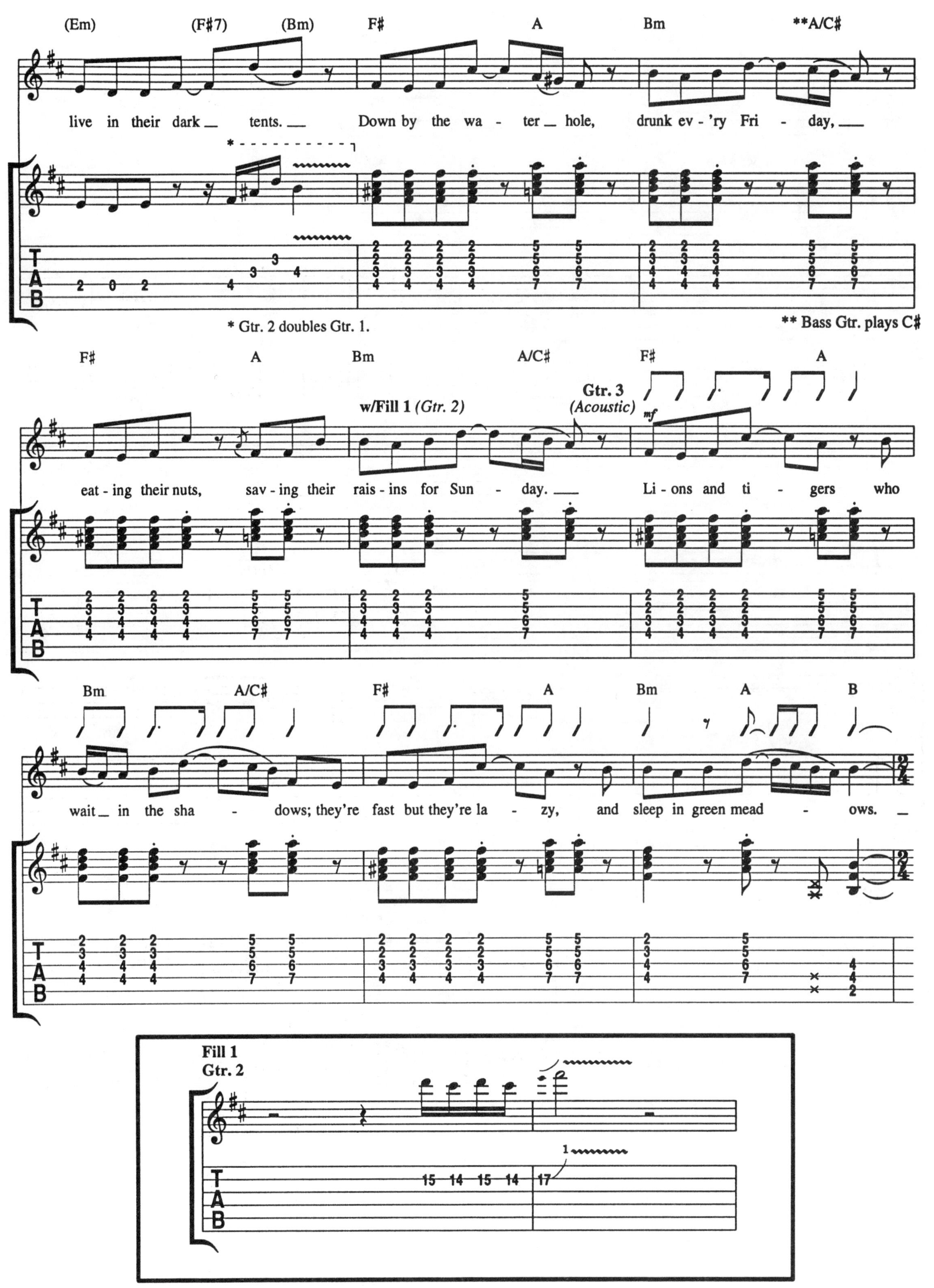
(Em) (F#7) (Bm) F# A Bm **A/C#
live in their dark _ tents. _ Down by the wa - ter _ hole, drunk ev - 'ry Fri - day, _
* Gr. 2 doubles Gtr. 1.
** Bass Gtr. plays C#
F# A Bm A/C# F# A
w/Fill 1 (Gtr. 2)
Gtr. 3 (Acoustic)
mf
eat - ing their nuts, sav - ing their rais - ins for Sun - day. _ Li - ons and ti - gers who
Bm A/C# F# A Bm A B
wait _ in the sha - dows; they're fast but they're la - zy, and sleep in green mead - ows. _
Fill 1
Gtr. 2

Chorus:
Rhy. Fig. 1
To Coda
G
A
D
Well, let's bun - gle in the jun - gle; well, that's
Rhy. Fig. 1A
w/Fill 2 (Gtr. 2, 2nd time)
G A B A B G A D
al - right by me, yes. Well, I'm a ti - ger when I want
G A
love; I'm a snake if we dis -
hold
Fill 2
Gtr. 2

1.
B
(end Rhy. Fig. 1)
2. w/Fill 3 (Gtr. 2)
B
a - gree.
gree,
yes.
(end Rhy. Fig. 1A)
Interlude:
Gtr. 3
(Acoustic)
*N.C. (Bm)
(A)
(Bm/F♯)
(Bm)
(A)
* Chords implied by Gtr. voicings & Bass Gtr.
Gtr. 4 (Acoustic)
(Bm/F♯)
(Bm)
(A)
(Bm/F♯)
mf
Gtr. 3
(Bm)
(A)
(Bm/F♯)
(Bm)
(A)
* Gtr. 2
Gtr. 1
* Gtr's 3 & 4 tacet.
Fill 3
Gtr. 2

D.S. al Coda
(Bm/F#)
(Bm)
(A)
(Bm/F#)
3. The
Coda
Chorus:
w/Rhy. Figs. 1 (Gtr. 3) & 1A (Gtr. 1) both until end.
G
A
D
B
bun - gle in the jun - gle; well, that's al - right by me,
yes. I'm a ti - ger when I want love, and I'm a
Gtr. 2
snake when we dis - a - gree, yeah. Let's bun - gle in the jun -

Verse 2:

Just say a word and the boys will be right there,
With claws at your back to send a chill through the night air.
Is it so frightening to have me at your shoulder?
Thunder and lightening couldn't be bolder.
I'll write on your tombstone, "I thank you for dinner."
This game that we animals play is a winner.

(To Chorus:)

Verse 3:

The rivers are full of crocodile nasties,
And He who made kittens put snakes in the grass.
He's a lover of life but a player of pawns.
Yes, the king on his sunset lies waiting for dawn
To light up his jungle as play is resumed;
The monkeys seem willing to strike up the tune.

(To Chorus:)

CROSS-EYED MARY

Words and Music by
IAN ANDERSON

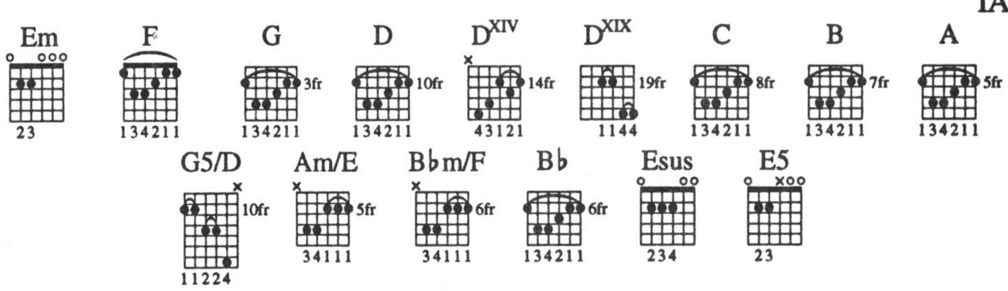

Moderate rock ♩=84

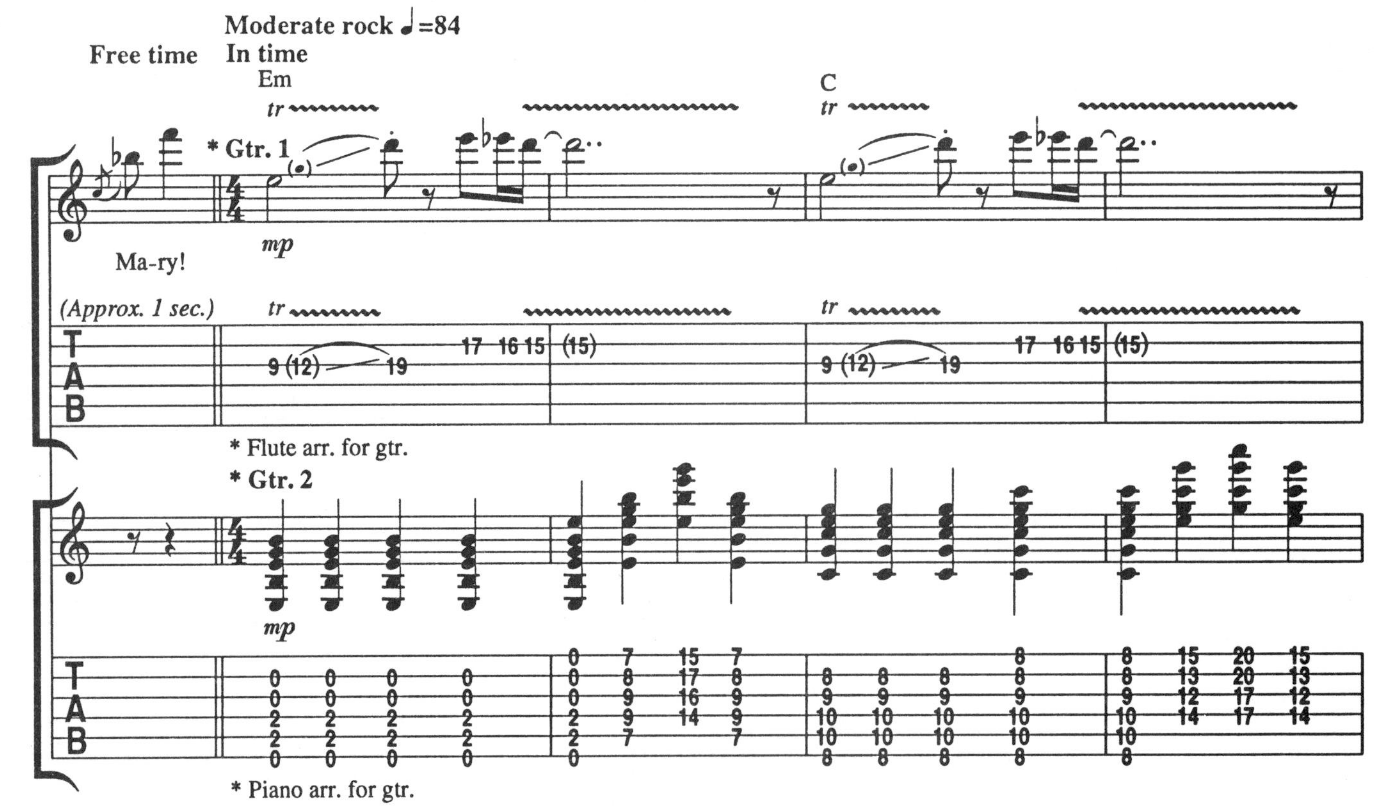

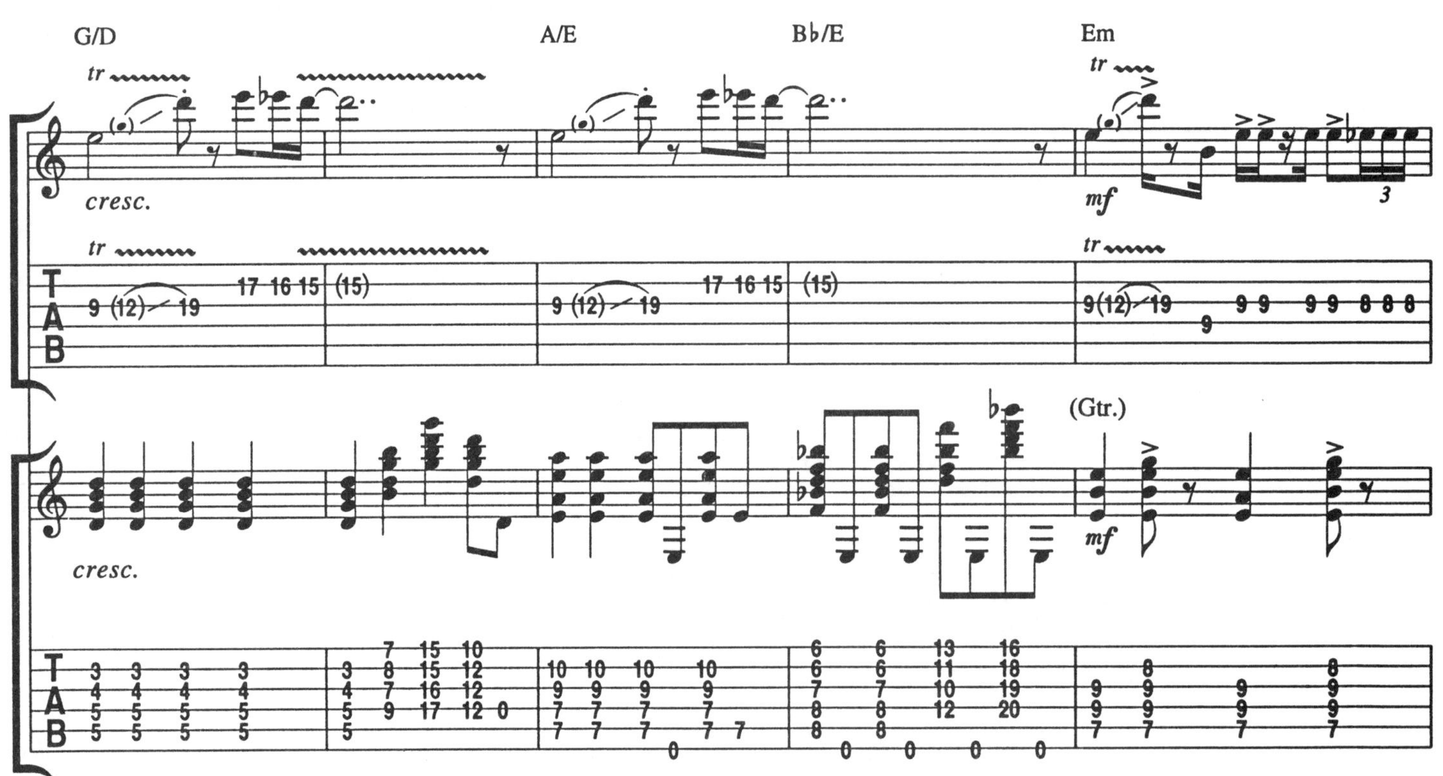

Bb Em Bb

C Ab D

C Cm Bb

(Piano & gtr., arr. for gtr.)

Verse 1:
Rhy. Fig. 1A
A
Esus
Em
tr
Gtr. 2 (piano)
1. Who would be a poor man, a
Rhy. Fig. 1
Gtr. 1 (elec. gtr.)
(w/heavy distortion)
(end Rhy. Fig. 1A)
F
G
D
beg-gar man a thief,
if he had a rich man in his
hand?
(end Rhy. Fig. 1)
w/Rhy. Figs. 1 & 1A
And who would s-steal the can - dy from a laugh-ing ba - by's mouth
if he could take it from the mon-ey
Chorus:
N.C.(Am)
G5
man?
Cross-eyed Mar - y,
a-goes
jump - ing in
a-gain.
She
Rhy. Fig. 2
* Gtrs. 1 & 2
* Piano & gtr.

N.C. (Am)
G5
N.C.(Am)
G5
N.C. (B♭m)
A♭5
signs no con - tract, but she al-ways plays the game. She dines in Hamp - stead Vil-lage on ex -
N.C. (B♭m)
A♭5
N.C. (B♭m)
A♭5
Rhy. Fig. 2A
C
Gtr. 2
pense ac-count-ed gruel. And the jack knife bar - ber drops her off at school.
Rhy. Fig. 2B
Gtr. 1
(end Rhy. Fig. 2)
2nd time to Coda
Verse 2:
(end Rhy. Fig. 2A)
w/Rhy. Fig. 1 (2 times)
D
C
B A B
Em
F
Hey! 2. Laugh - ing in the play ground, gets no kicks from lit - tle boys, would
(end Rhy. Fig. 2B)
Rhy. Fig. 3
Gtr. 2 (piano)

G
D
w/Rhy. Fig. 3
Em
rath-er make it with a letch-ing grey.
(end Rhy. Fig. 3)
Or may-be her at-ten-tion is drawn
8va
F
G
D
by Aq-ua-lung, who watch-es through the rail-ings as they play.
Hey!
Chorus:
w/Rhy. Fig. 2
N.C.(Am)
G5
Cross-eyed Mar-y finds it hard to get a-long.
She's a poor man's rich girl and she'll
N.C. (Am)
Ab5
N.C. (Bbm)
do it for a song.
She's a rich man s-steal-er, but her fa-vour's good and strong.
She's the
w/Rhy. Figs. 2A & 2B
C
D C
B A B
Rob-in Hood of High-gate, helps the poor man get a-long, ah!
Hey!
Flute solo: (arr. for gtr.)
w/Rhy. Fig. 2
(steady gliss)
* These notes are sung through the flute.

N.C.(B♭m)
A♭5
N.C.(B♭m)
A♭5
1/2
1
N.C. (B♭m)
A♭5
w/Rhy. Fig. 2A
C
D
C
D
B A
B
1
1/2
1
Verse 3:
Rhy. Fig. 1A (2 times)
Em
F
Laugh - ing in the play _ ground, _ gets no _ kicks from lit - tle boys, _ would
Gtr. 1
mf
G
D
D^XIV
D^XIX
Em
rath - er make it with _ a _ letch - ing grey. _
Or may - be her at - ten - tion is drawn _
D.S. 𝄋 al Coda
F
G
D
D^XIV
D^XIX
_ by _ Aq - ua - lung, _ who watch - es through the rail - ings _ as _ they _ play. _
Hey!

Coda
Gtr. 2 (piano)
C
Em
Cross - eyed Mar - y.
Gtr. 1 (flute)
G5/D
Am/E
Bbm/F
F
Db
(Gtr.)
8va
loco
Em
Bb
C
D
Oh, Mar - y!
poco rit.
Oh,
(Flute)
Free time
Esus
E5
oh, Cross-eyed Mar - y.
Yeow!

LIFE IS A LONG SONG

Words and Music by
IAN ANDERSON

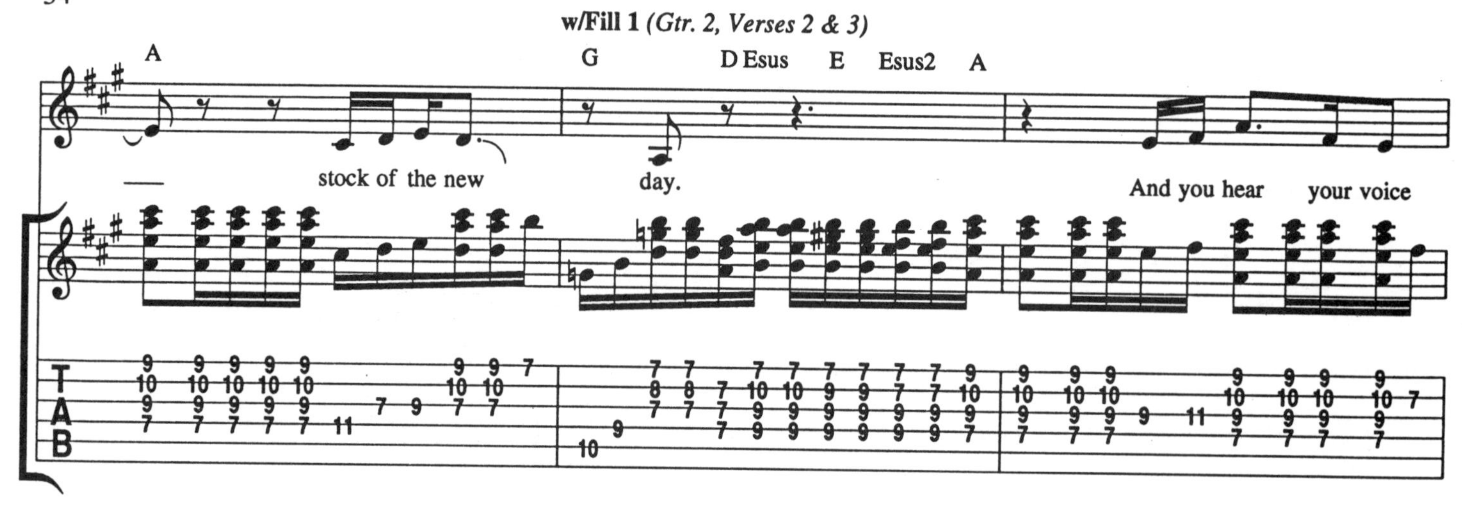
w/Fill 1 (Gtr. 2, Verses 2 & 3)
A
G
D Esus
E
Esus2
A
stock of the new
day.
And you hear your voice

w/Fill 2 (Gtr. 2, Verses 2 & 3)
G/A
D6
A
G
D Esus
E
D C
croak
as you choke
on what you need to
say.

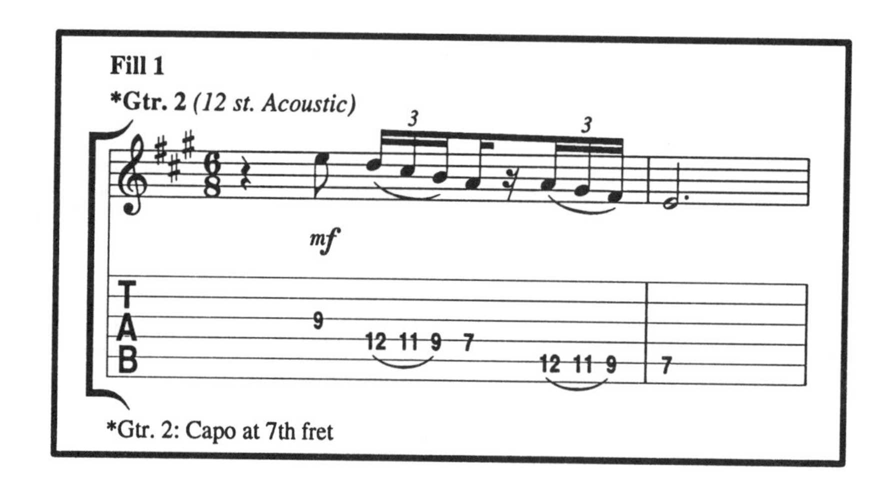
Fill 1
*Gtr. 2 (12 st. Acoustic)
mf
*Gtr. 2: Capo at 7th fret

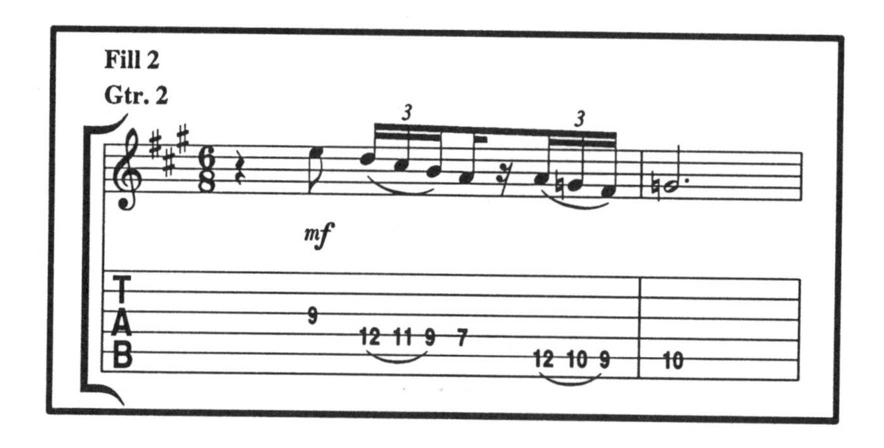
Fill 2
Gtr. 2
mf

Csus2 C
G
D D/F#
D
Well don't you fret, don't you fear, I will give you good
T
A
B

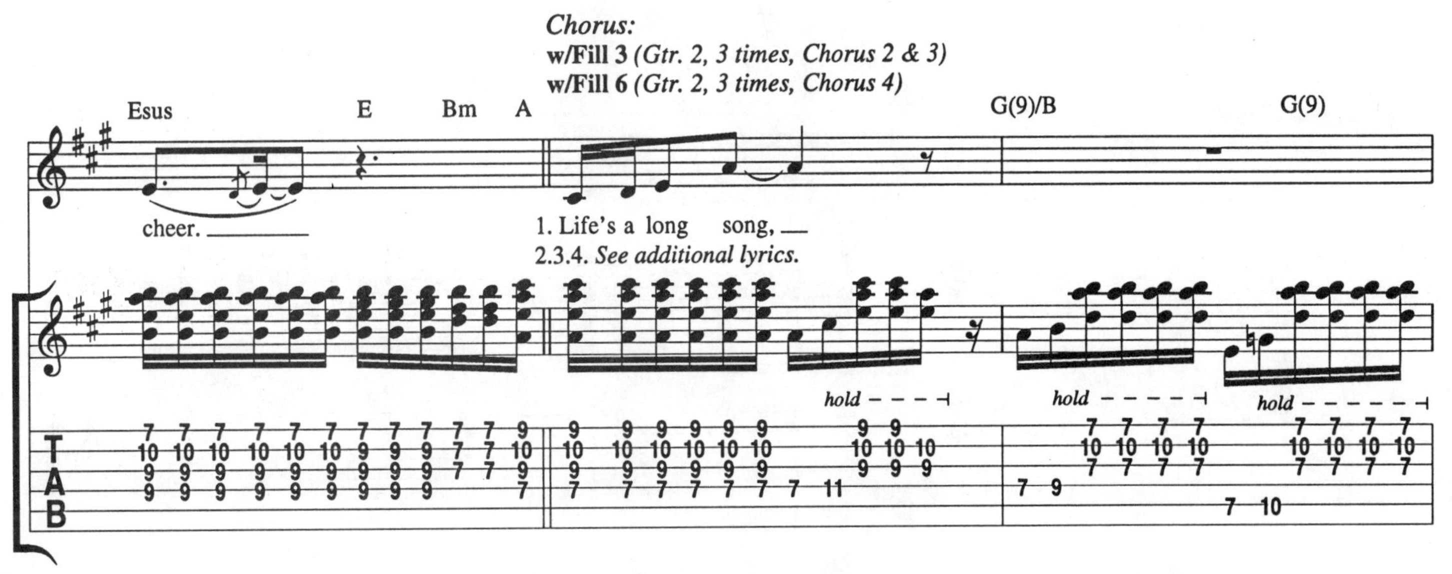
Chorus:
w/Fill 3 (Gtr. 2, 3 times, Chorus 2 & 3)
w/Fill 6 (Gtr. 2, 3 times, Chorus 4)
Esus
E
Bm
A
G(9)/B
G(9)
cheer.
1. Life's a long song,
2.3.4. See additional lyrics.
hold
hold
hold
T
A
B

Fill 3
Gtr. 2
T
A
B

Fill 6
Gtr. 2
T
A
B

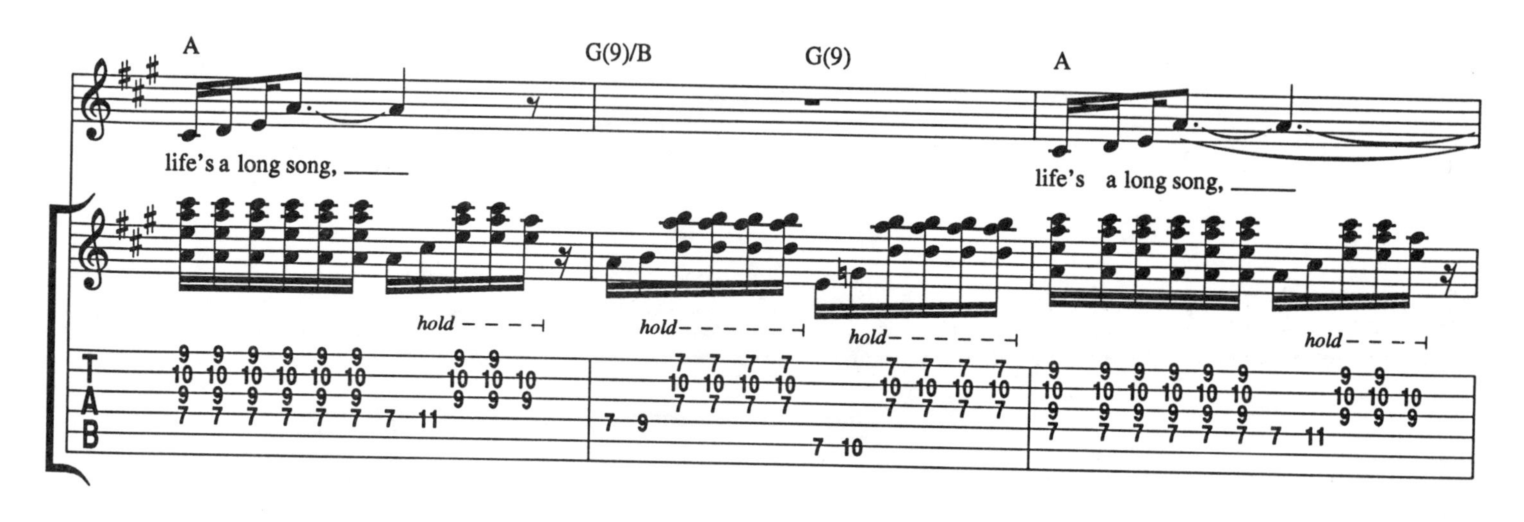
A
G(9)/B
G(9)
A
life's a long song,
life's a long song,
hold
hold
hold
hold

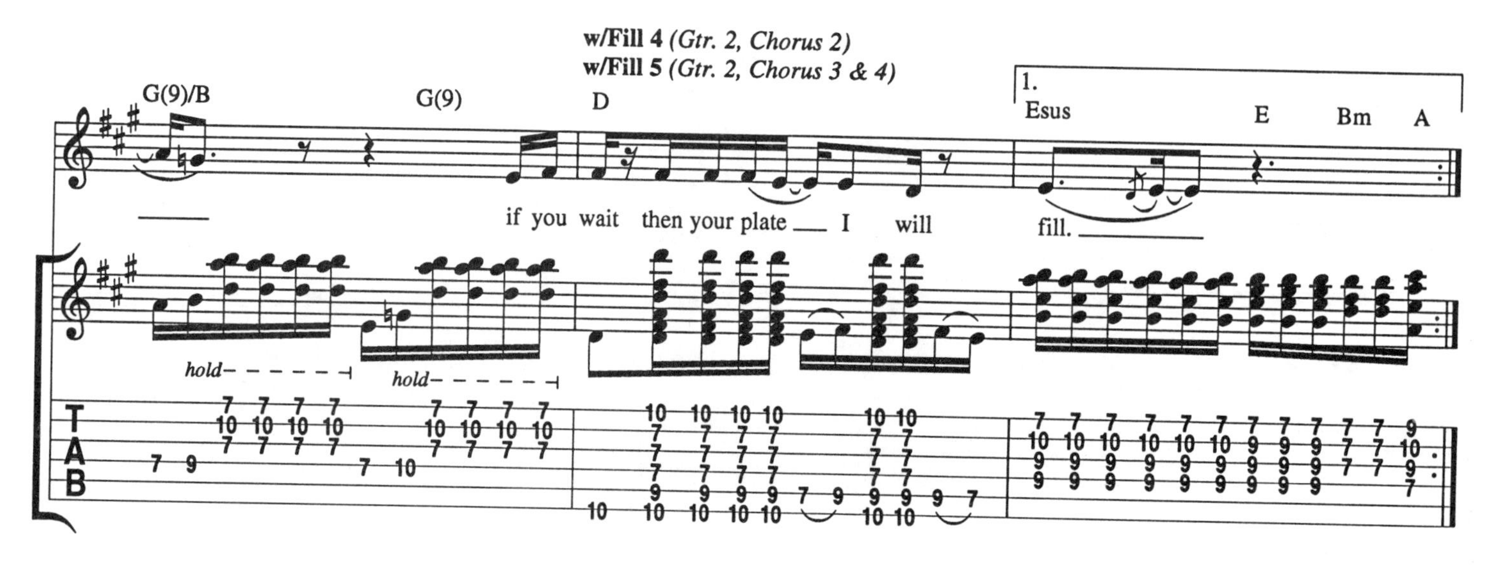
w/Fill 4 (Gtr. 2, Chorus 2)
w/Fill 5 (Gtr. 2, Chorus 3 & 4)
G(9)/B
G(9)
D
1.
Esus
E
Bm
A
if you wait then your plate I will
fill.
hold
hold

Fill 4
Gtr. 2

Fill 5
Gtr. 2

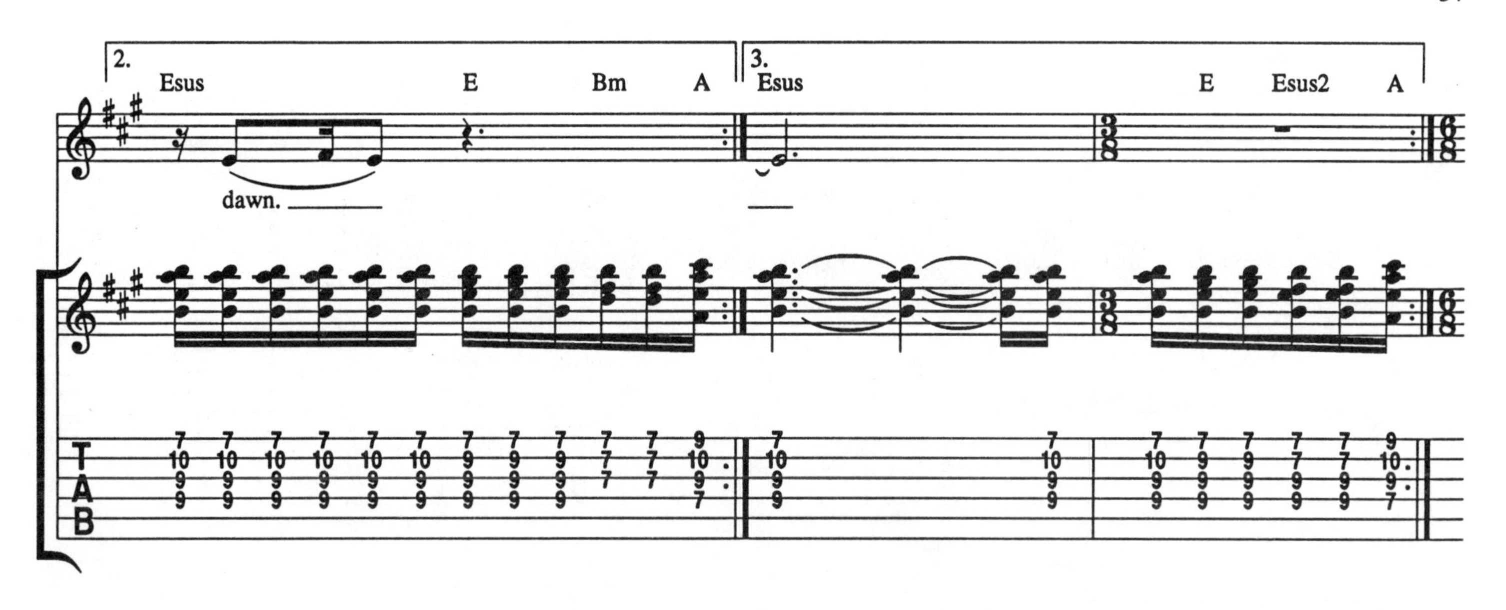

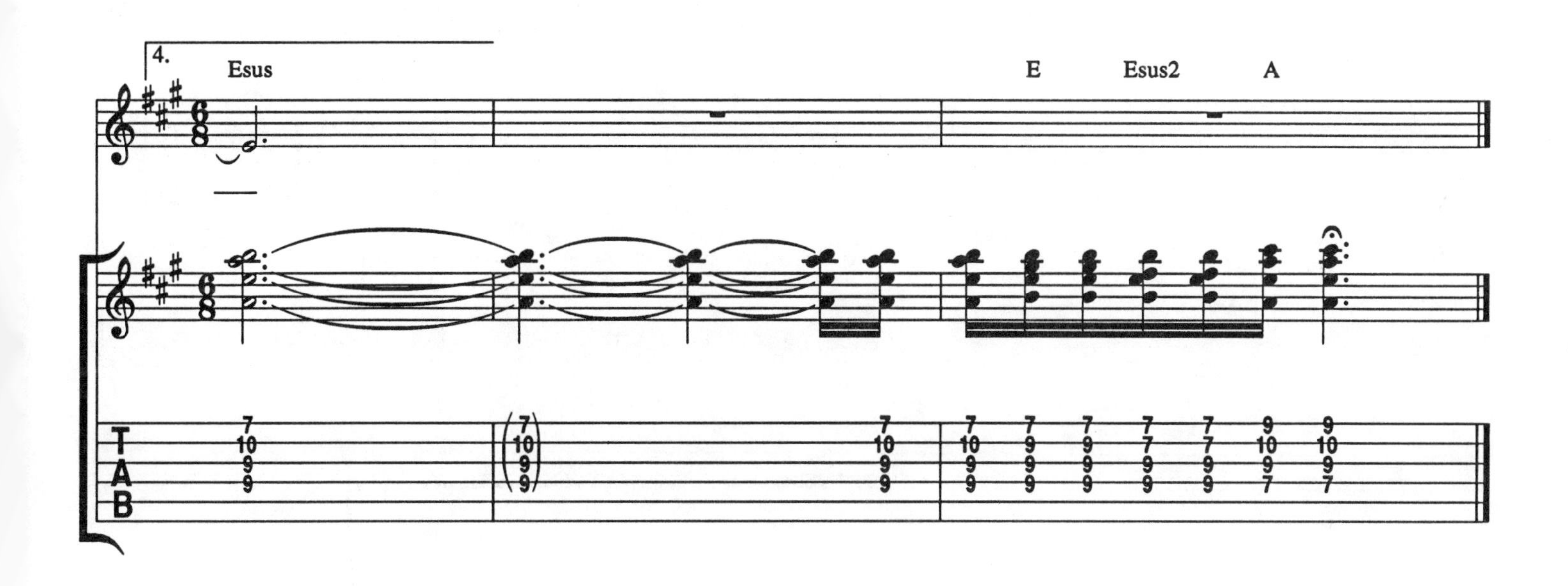

Verse 2:

As the verses unfold and your soul
Suffers the long day.
And the twelve o'clock gloom spins the room,
You struggle on your way.
Well don't you sigh, don't you cry
Lick dust from your eye.
(To Chorus:)

Chorus 2:

Life's a long song,
Life's a long song,
Life's a long song.
We will meet in the sweet light of dawn.
(To Verse 3:)

Verse 3:

As the Baker street train
Spills your pain all over your new dress,
And the symphony sounds under ground
Put you under duress,
Well don't you squeal
As the heel grinds you under the wheels.
(To Chorus:)

Chorus 3:

Life's a long song,
Life's a long song,
Life's a long song.
But the tune ends too soon for us all.
(To Verse 4:)

Verse 4:

Instrumental
(To Chorus:)

Chorus 4:

Instrumental (con't.)
But the tune ends too soon for us all.

LIVING IN THE PAST

Words and Music by
IAN ANDERSON

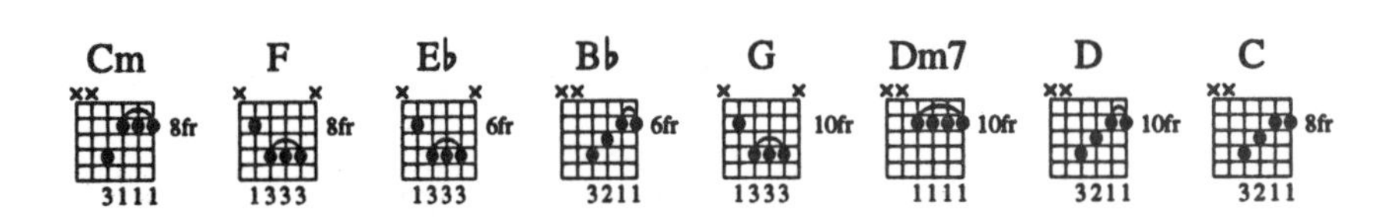

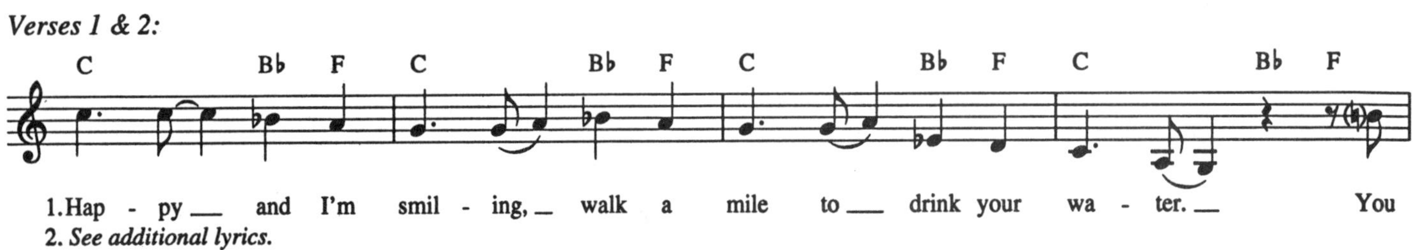

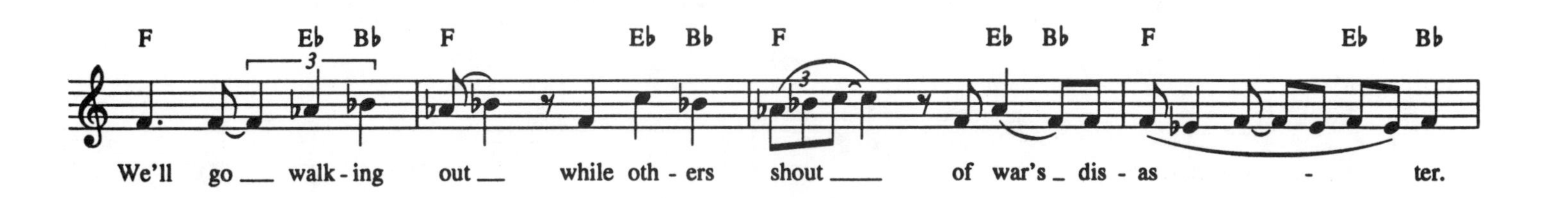

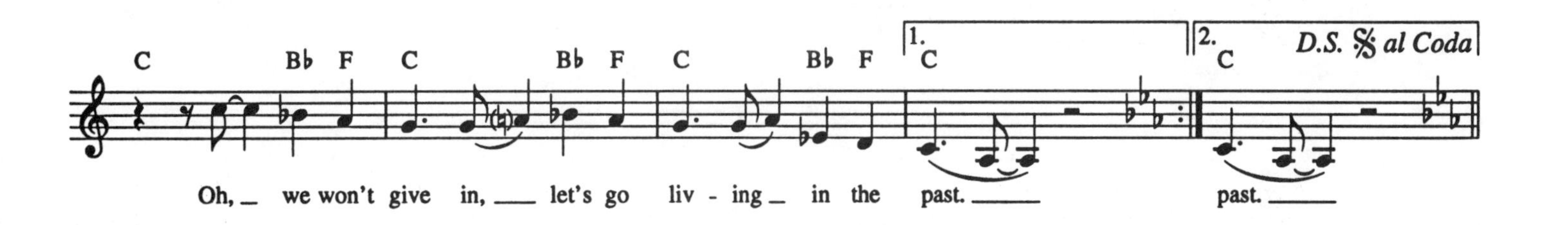

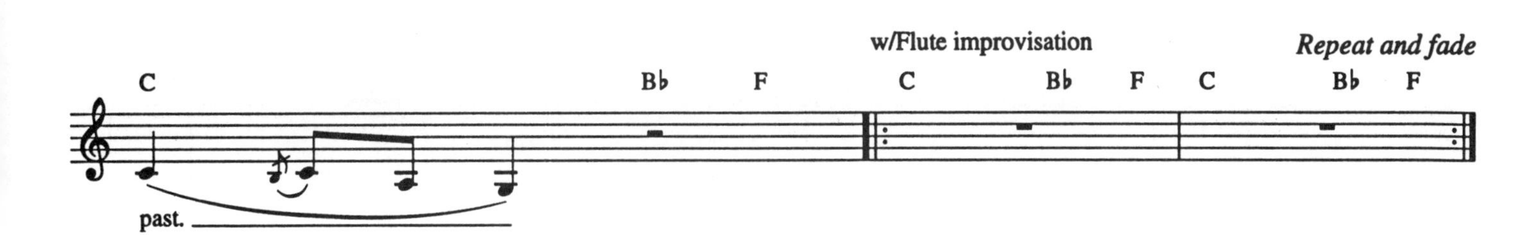

Verse 2:

Once I used to join in,
Every boy and girl was my friend.
Now there's revolution
But they don't know what they're fighting.
Let us close our eyes;
Outside their lives go on much faster.
Oh, we won't give in,
We'll keep living in the past.

(To Intro:)

LOCOMOTIVE BREATH

Words and Music by
IAN ANDERSON

w/Fill 2
Tempo I ♩=152
w/Improv. piano
Em
G
D
A.H.
(15ma)
Fill 2
Gtr. 1

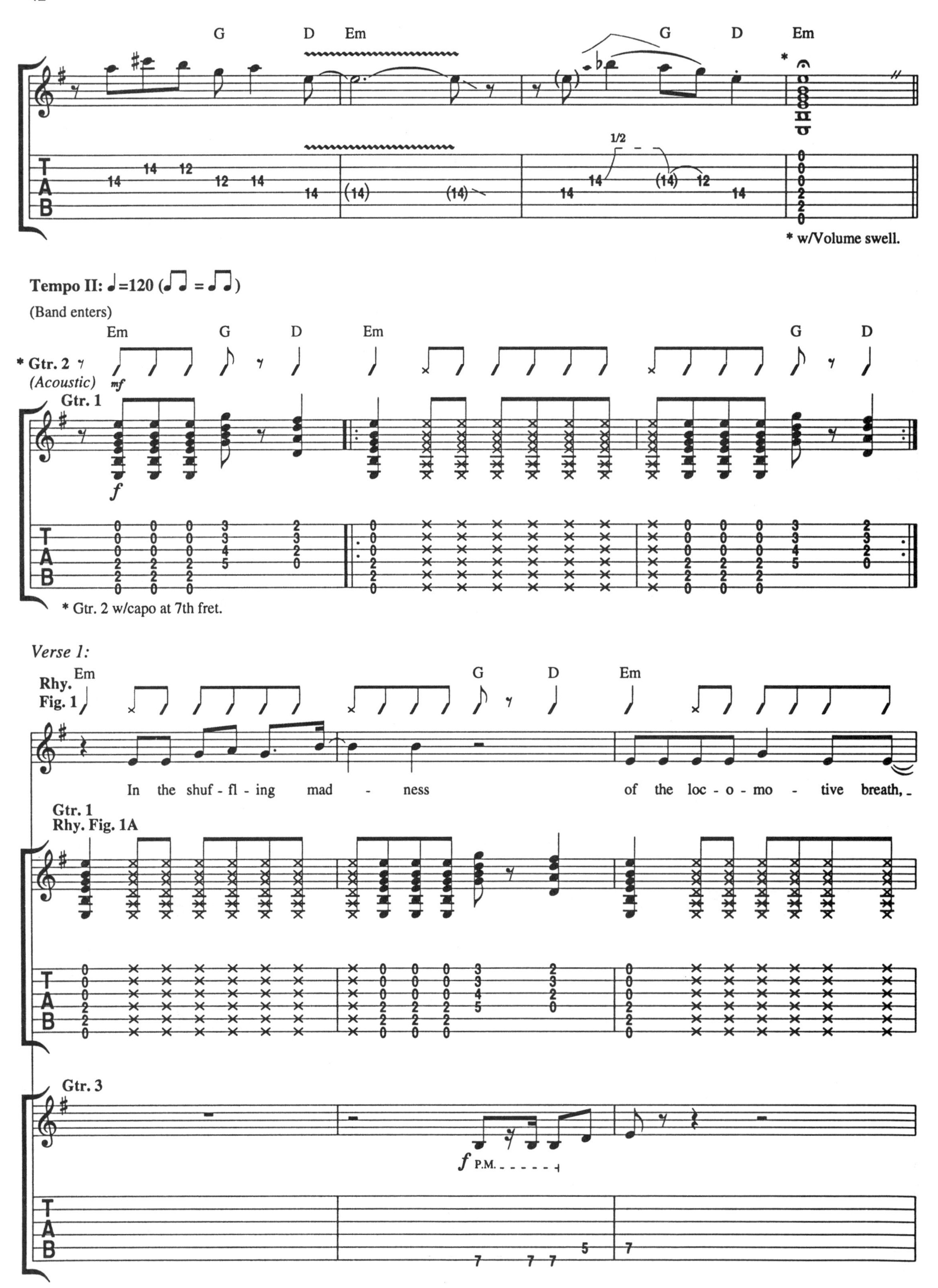
G
D
Em
G
D
Em
1/2
* w/Volume swell.
Tempo II: ♩=120
(Band enters)
Em
G
D
Em
G
D
* Gtr. 2
(Acoustic)
mf
Gtr. 1
f
* Gtr. 2 w/capo at 7th fret.
Verse 1:
Rhy. Fig. 1
Em
G
D
Em
In the shuf - fl - ing mad - ness of the loc - o - mo - tive breath,
Gtr. 1
Rhy. Fig. 1A
Gtr. 3
f
P.M.

Em
G
D
Em
G
D
runs the all time los - er,
B
D
Em
head - long to his death.
Oh, he feels the pis - ton scrap -

G
D
Em
G
D
- ing,
steam
break - ing on his brow.
Old
w/Fills 1(Gtr. 4) & 1A(Gtr. 5)
G
A
B
Char - lie stole the han - dle,
and the train, it won't stop

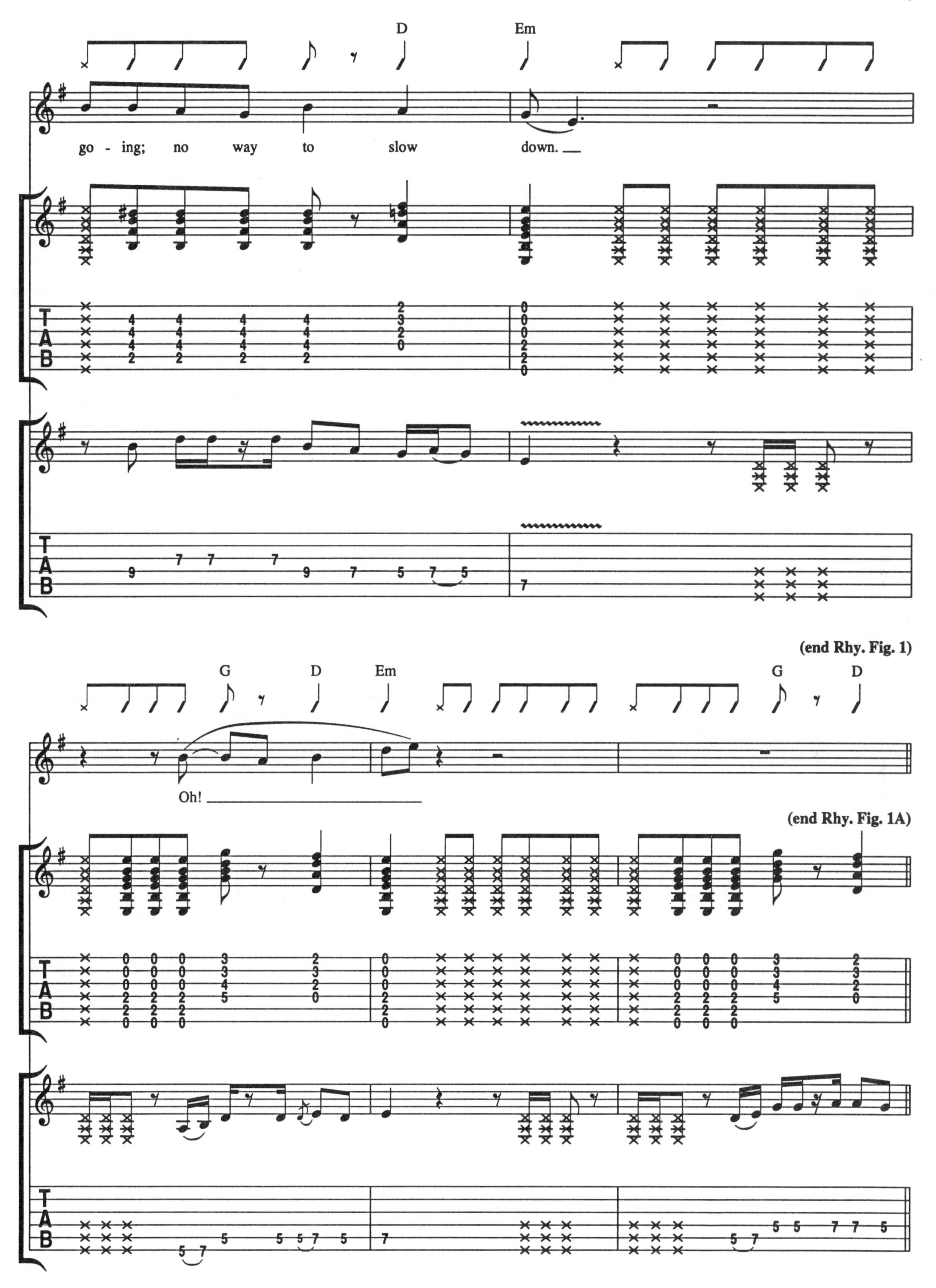
D
Em
go - ing; no way to slow down.
T
A
B
(end Rhy. Fig. 1)
G
D
Em
G
D
Oh!
(end Rhy. Fig. 1A)

Verse 2:
w/Rhy. Figs. 1 (Gtr. 2) & 1A (Gtr. 1)

Em
G
D
Em
He sees his chil-dren jump - ing off
at sta - tions, one by
Gtr. 3
one;
His wom - an and his best friend,
P.M.
B
in bed and hav - ing fun.
Oh, he's crawl - ing down the cor - ri -
dor
on his hands and knees.
Old
P.M.
TAB

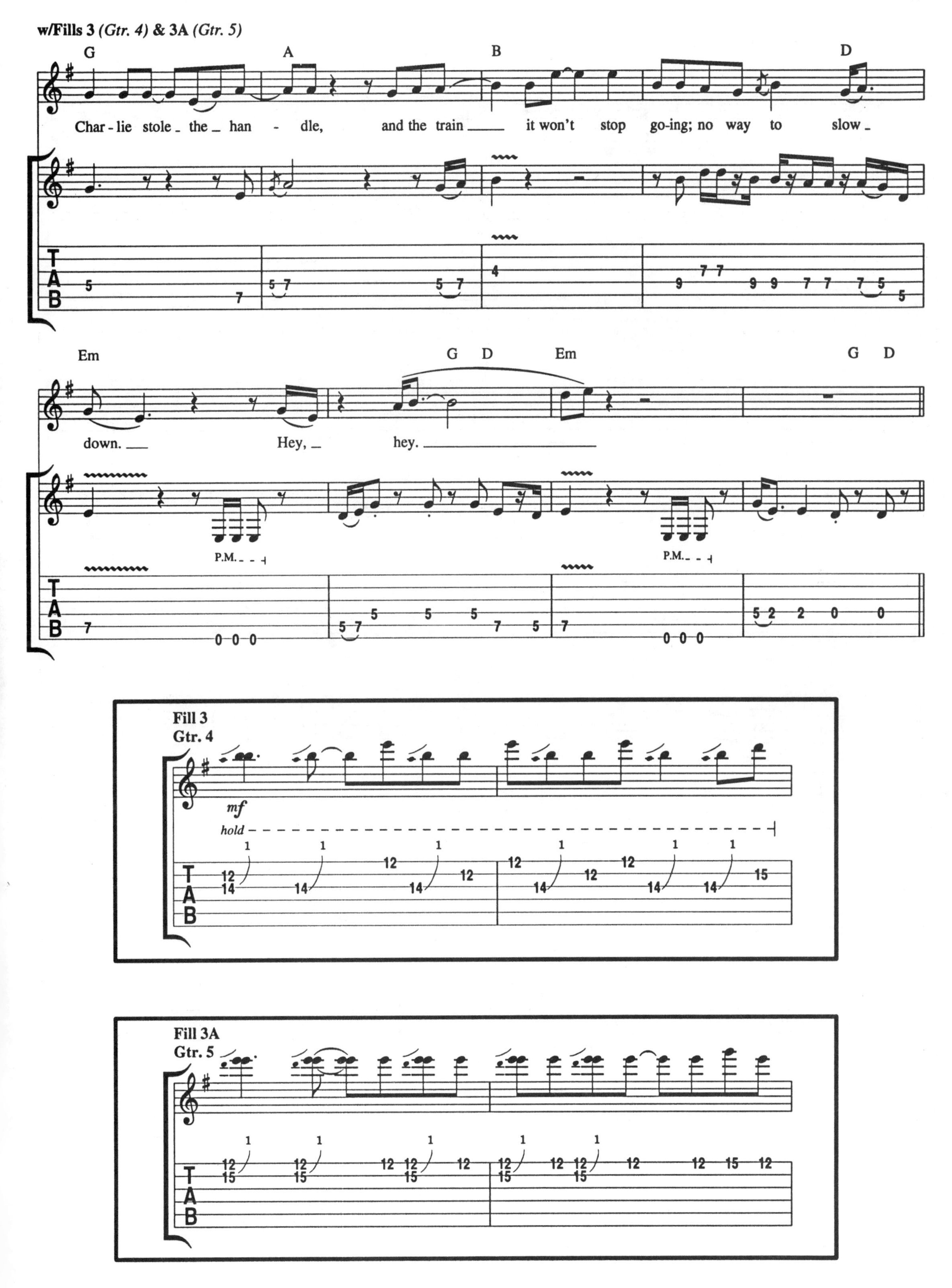
w/Fills 3 (Gtr. 4) & 3A (Gtr. 5)
G
A
B
D
Char - lie stole the han - dle, and the train it won't stop go-ing; no way to slow
Em
G D
Em
G D
down. Hey, hey.
P.M.
P.M.
Fill 3
Gtr. 4
mf
hold
Fill 3A
Gtr. 5

Flute Solo:
w/Rhy.Figs. 1 (Gtr. 2) & 1A (Gtr. 1)
Em
G
D
Em
G
D
P.M.
B
w/Fills 3 (Gtr. 4) & 3A (Gtr. 5)
A

Verse 3:

w/Rhy. Figs. 1 *(Gtr. 2)* & 1A *(Gtr. 1)*

Em G D Em

He hears the si - lence howl - ing, __ catch - es an - gels __ as they

G D Em G D

fall, __ and the all - time win - ner ______

B D Em

has got him __ by __ the balls. _____ Oh, __ he picks up Gid - 'on's Bi -

P.M.

G D Em G D

- ble, o - pen at page __ one. __ I thank

w/Fills 3 (Gtr. 4) & 3A (Gtr. 5)
substitute w/Rhythm Fills 1 (Gtr. 2) & 1A (Gtr. 1)
G
A
B
God he stole the han - dle, and the train it won't stop
1/4
1/4
D
Em
G
D
go-ing; no way to slow down. No way to slow
Em
w/Rhy. Figs. 1 (Gtr. 2) &1A (Gtr. 1)
1st 2 bars only until end.
G
D
Em
down. No way to slow down.
Rhy. Fill 1 (Gtr. 2)
B
Rhy. Fill 1A (Gtr. 1)

G
D
Em
No way to slow down.
P.M.
G
D
Em
No way to slow down.
1/4
1/4
G
D
Em
No way to slow down.
G
D
Em
Fade
No way to slow down.

MINSTREL IN THE GALLERY

Words and Music by
IAN ANDERSON
(Some Music by
MARTIN BARRE)

(E5)
Verses 1 & 3:
Esus
E
A5
B
1. The min - strel in the gal - ler - y
Rhy. Fig. 1
3. See additional lyrics.
G5
D
Esus
looked down up - on the smil - ing fac - es.
(end Rhy. Fig. 1)
w/Rhy. Fig. 1 (Gtr. 1, 2 times)
E
A5
B
G5
D
He met the ga - zes, ob - served the spa - ces, in - be - tween the old
Esus
E
A5
B
men's cack - le. And he brewed a song of love and ha -

w/Rhy. Fig. 1 (Gtr. 1, 1st 3 bars only)
G5 D Esus E
tred, o-blique sug-ges - tions and he wait - ed. He po - lar-ized
A5 B G5 D
the pump - kin eat - ers, stat - ic hum - ming,
A5 Esus E F♯sus
To Coda
pan - el beat - ers.
Gtr. 1
Chorus:
Bm E A5 F♯5 D E
The min - strel in the gal - ler - y looked down on the rab-bit.
Rhy. Fig. 2
Gtr. 1
hold
Gtr. 2

F♯5/C♯
D
E
run.
And he threw a - way his
A5
F♯5
D
E
look - ing glass,
and saw his face in ev' -

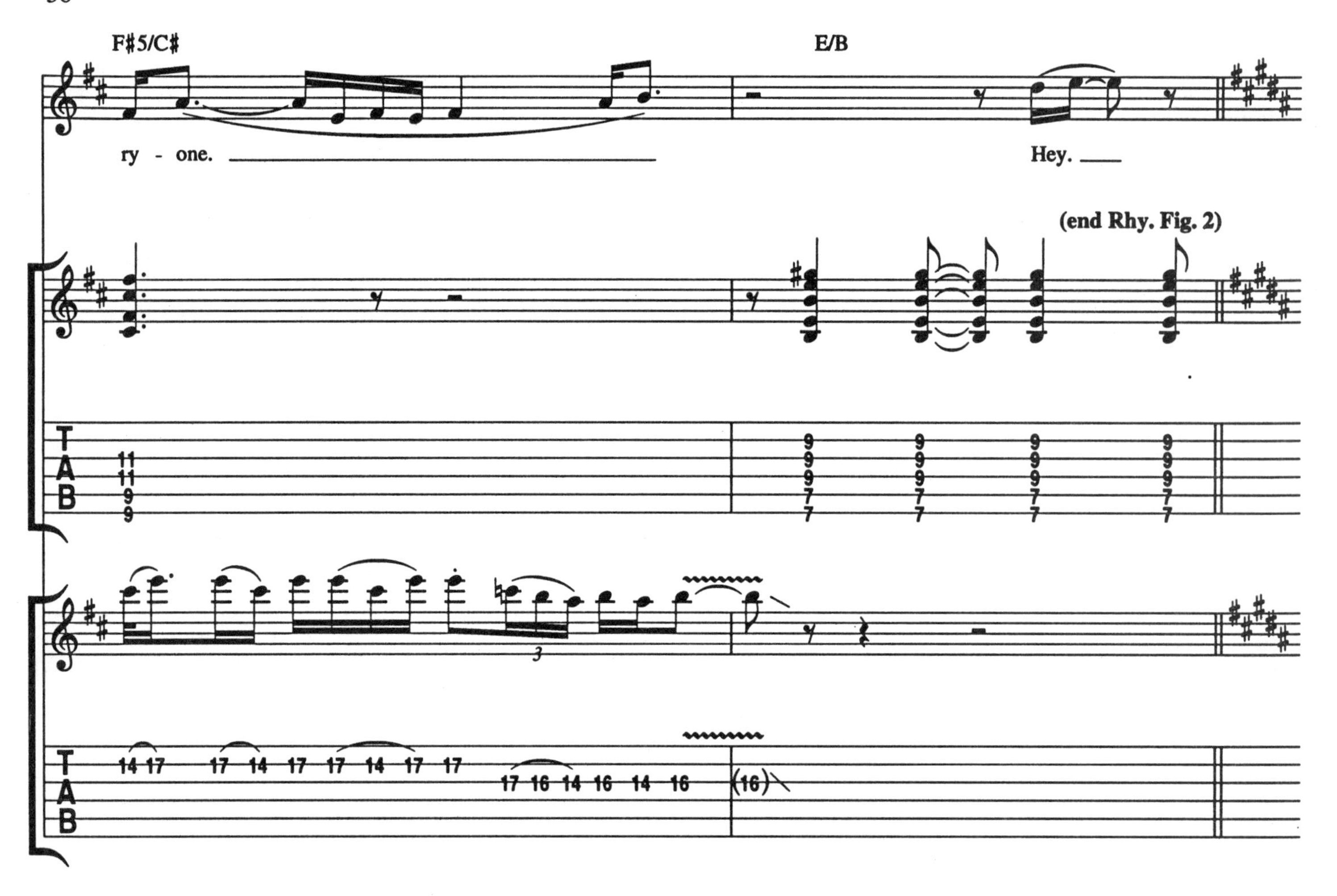

Verse 2:
w/Rhy. Fig. 1 (Gtr.1)

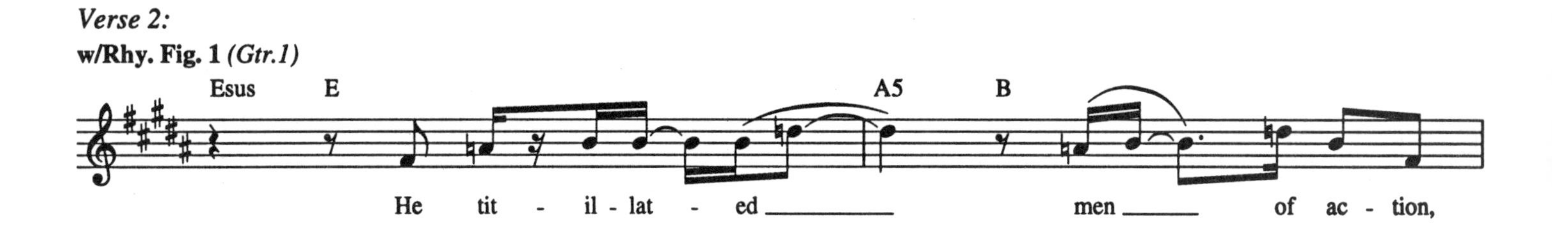

w/Rhy. Fig. 1 (Gtr. 1st 3 bars only)

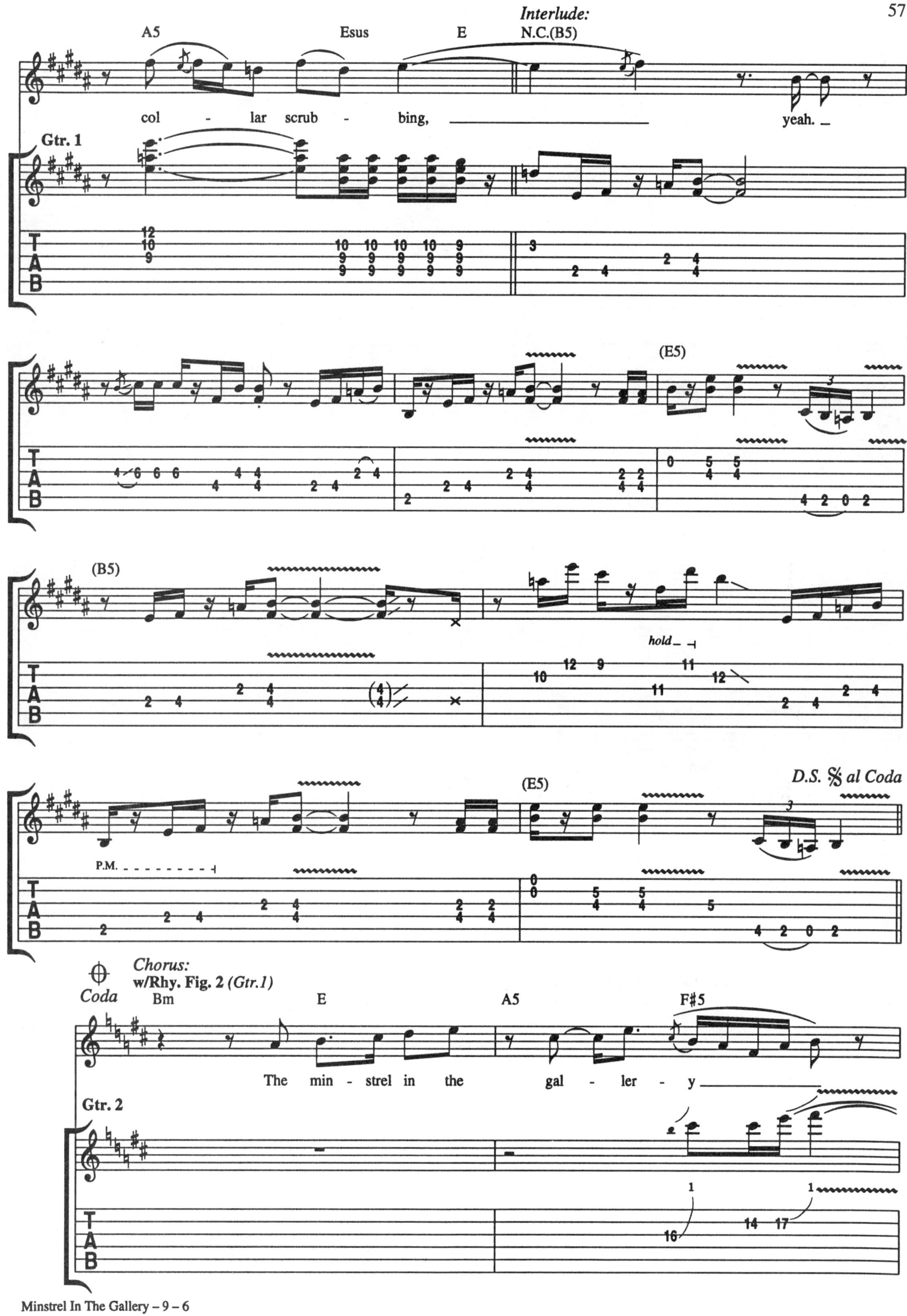
Interlude:
A5
Esus
E
N.C.(B5)
col - lar scrub - bing, yeah.
Gtr. 1
(E5)
(B5)
hold
P.M.
(E5)
D.S. 𝄋 al Coda
Coda
Chorus:
w/Rhy. Fig. 2 (Gtr.1)
Bm
E
A5
F#5
The min - strel in the gal - ler - y
Gtr. 2

D
E
F♯5/C♯
looked down on the rab - bit run.
D
E
A5
F♯5
Then he threw a - way his look - ing glass
D
E
F♯5/C♯
E/B
and saw his face in ev' - ry - one.
Hey.
hold
Outro:
N.C.(B5)
Gtr. 1

(E5)
The min - strel in the gal - ler -
(B5)
y, yeah, yeah,
hold
(E5)
looked down up - on the smil - ing fac -
(B5)
es.
hold
TAB

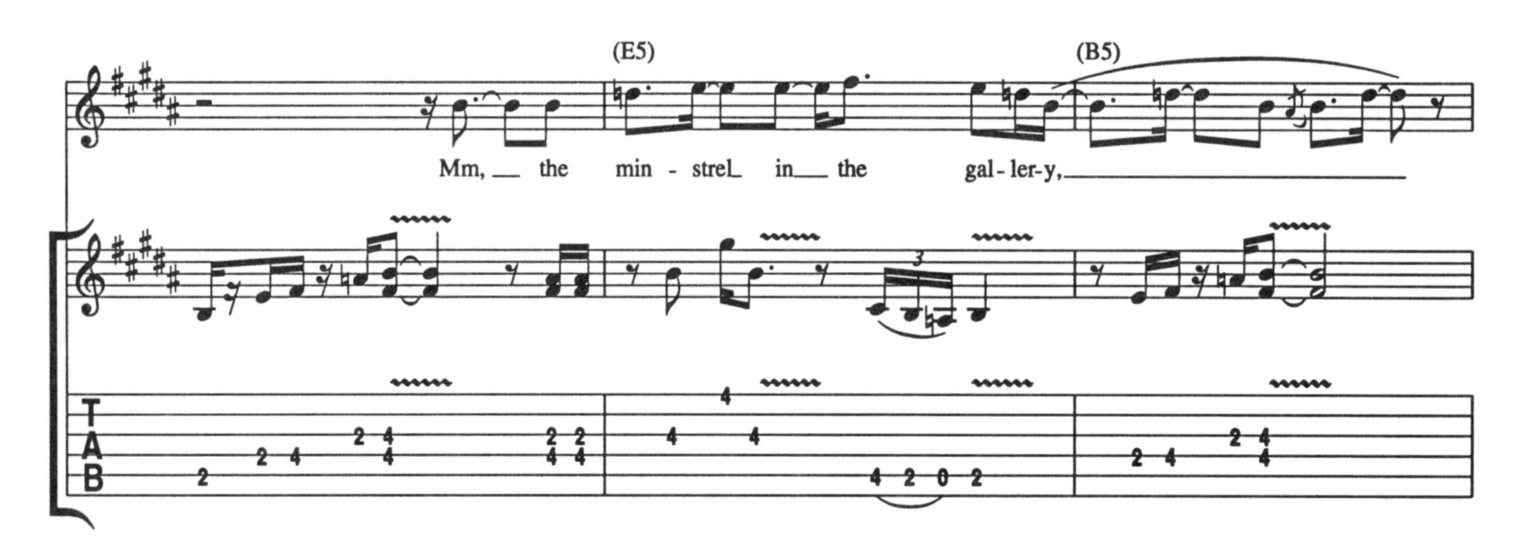

Verse 3:

He pacified the nappy suffering, infant-bleating one-line jokers,
T.V. documentary makers (overfed and undertakers).
Sunday paper backgammon players, family scarred and women haters.
Then he called the band down to the stage,
And he looked at all the friends he'd made.

(To Chorus:)

MOTHER GOOSE

Words and Music by
IAN ANDERSON

w/Flute Riff A (2 times, Verses 1 & 2)
w/Fill 1 (Gtr. 2, Verse 3)
Dsus2 C5 Am Dsus2 C5 Am
- ing.
D9(3) D5 F
And the for-eign stu - dent said to me, "Was it
G F G G5/F
real - ly true, that there are el - e-phants, li - ons too in Pic - ca-dil - ly
Fill 1
Gtr. 2 (Electric) D5
f

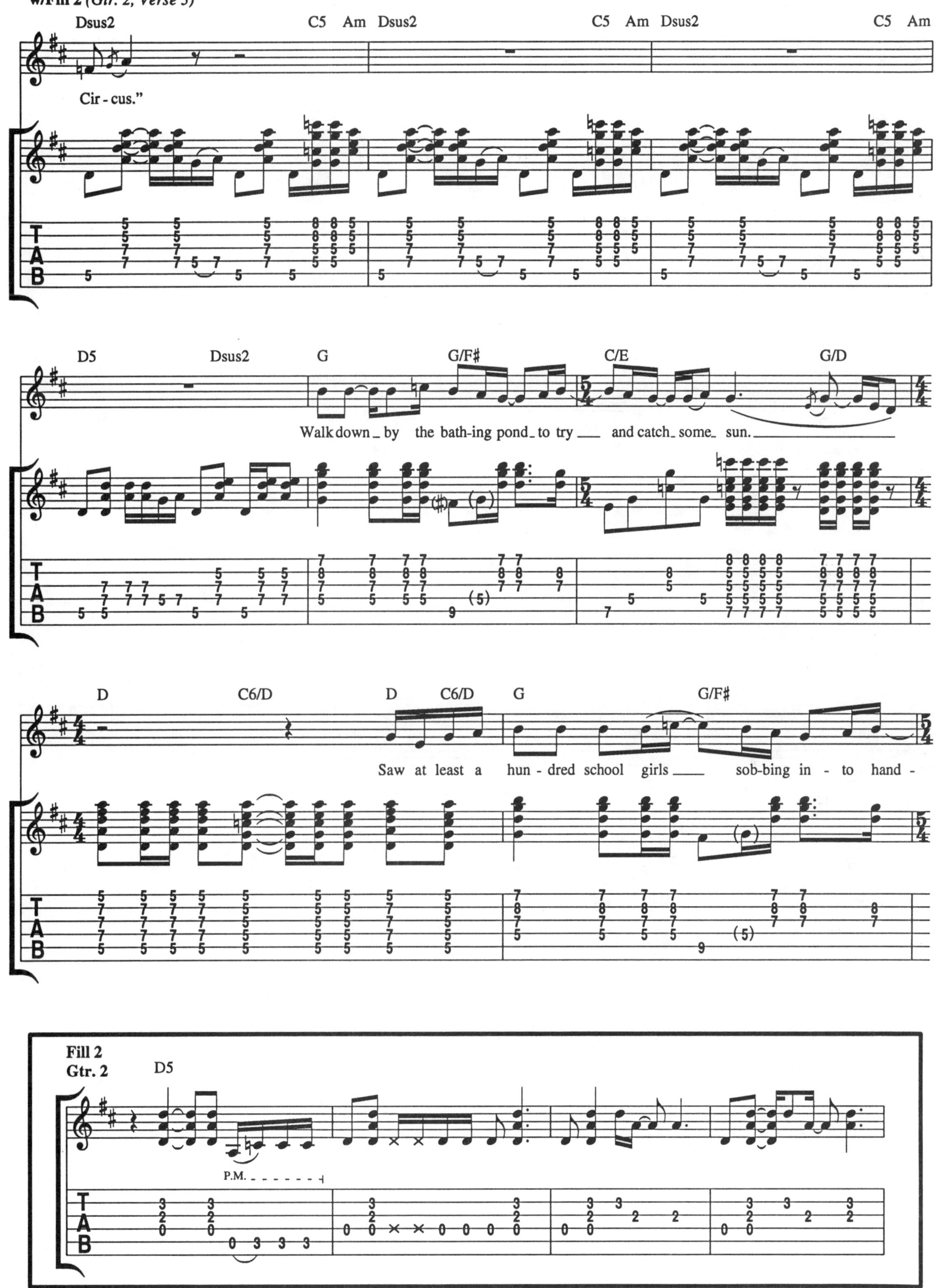
w/Flute Riff A (3 times, Verses 1 & 2)
w/Fill 2 (Gtr. 2, Verse 3)
Dsus2
C5 Am Dsus2
C5 Am Dsus2
C5 Am
Cir - cus."
D5
Dsus2
G
G/F#
C/E
G/D
Walk down _ by the bath-ing pond _ to try ___ and catch _ some _ sun. ___
D
C6/D
D C6/D
G
G/F#
Saw at least a hun - dred school girls ___ sob-bing in - to hand -
Fill 2
Gtr. 2
D5
P.M.

C/E
G/D
D
C6/D
D
C6/D
- ker - chiefs _ as ___ one. ___ I

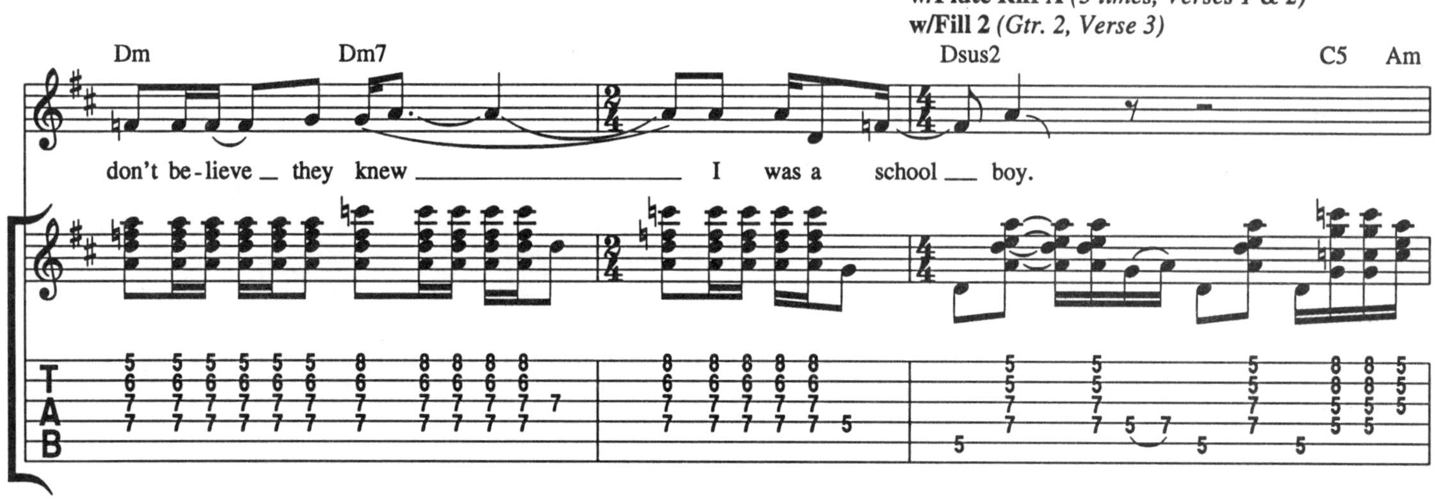
w/Flute Riff A (3 times, Verses 1 & 2)
w/Fill 2 (Gtr. 2, Verse 3)
Dm
Dm7
Dsus2
C5
Am
don't be - lieve _ they knew ___ I was a school ___ boy.

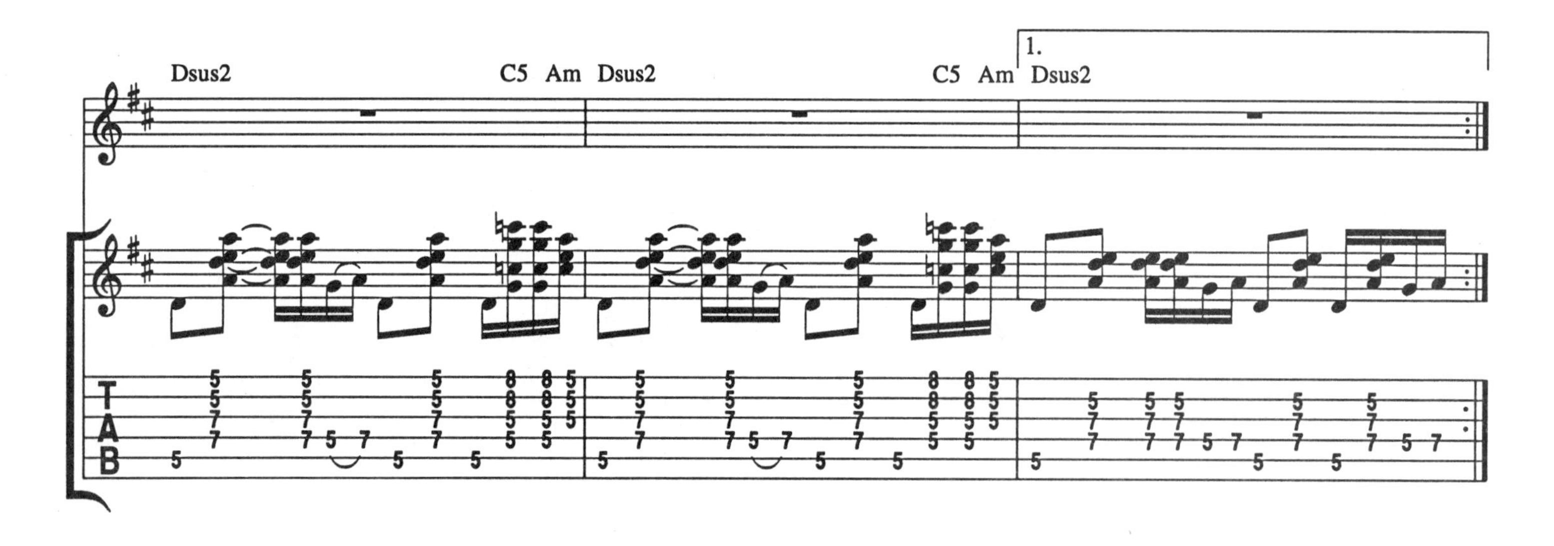
Dsus2
C5
Am
Dsus2
C5
Am
1.
Dsus2

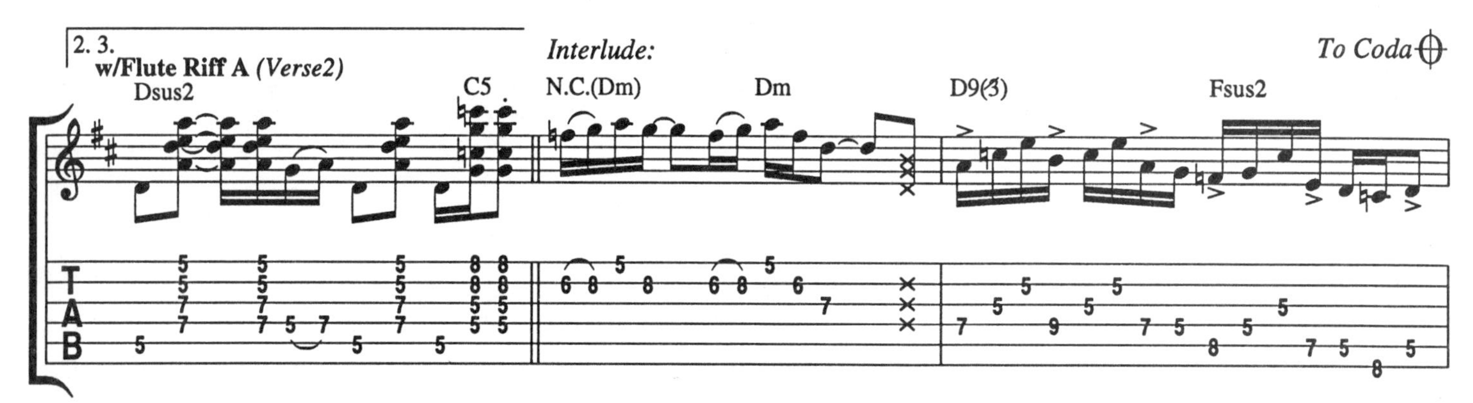
2. 3.
w/Flute Riff A (Verse2)
Dsus2
C5
Interlude:
N.C.(Dm)
Dm
D9(3)
Fsus2
To Coda

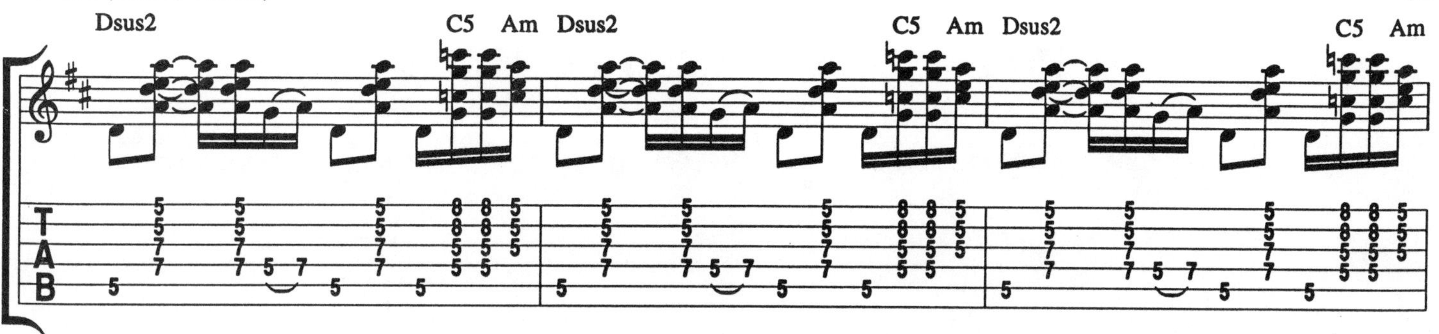

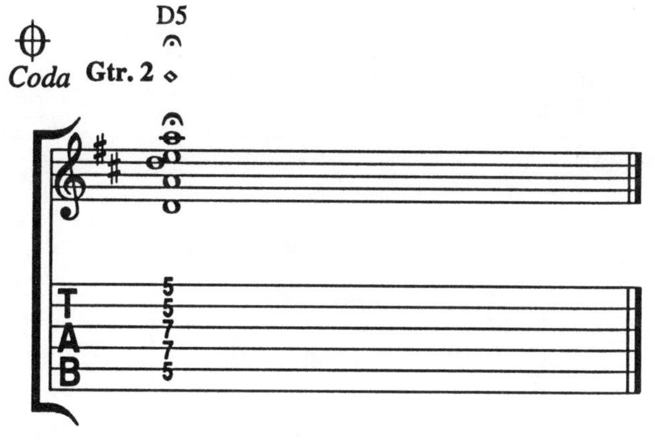

Verse 2:
And the bearded lady said to me
"If you start your raving and your misbehaving
You'll be sorry."
And the chicken fancier came to play
With his long red beard and his sister's wierd,
She drives a lorry.
Laughed down by the putting green,
I popped them in their holes.
Four and twenty labourers were laboring
And digging up their gold.
I don't believe they knew that I was Long John Silver.

(To Interlude:)

Verse 3:
Saw Johnny's scarecrow make his rounds
In his jet black mac'
Which he won't give back,
Stole it from a snowman.
As I did walk by past Hampstead Fair
I came upon Mother Goose,
So I turned her loose,
She was screaming.
Walked down by the bathing pond
To try and catch some sun.
Must have been at least a hundred school girls
Sobbing into handkerchiefs as one.
I don't believe they knew I was a school boy.

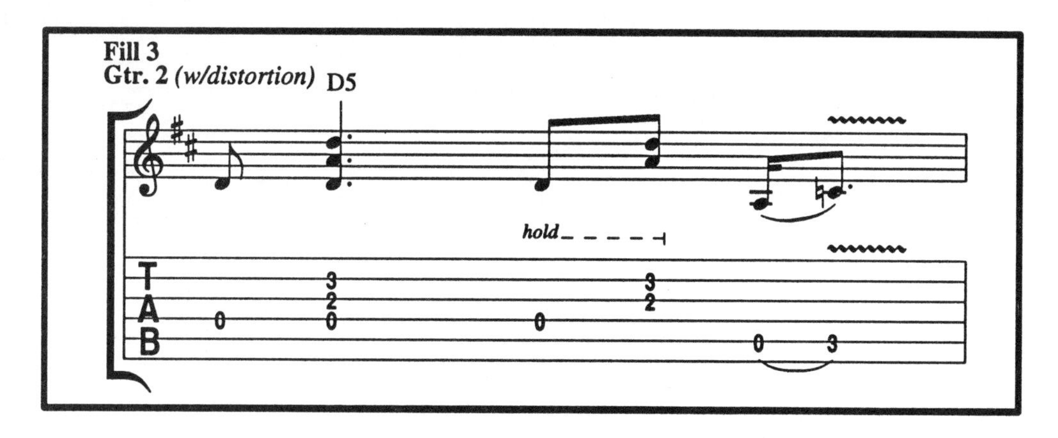

A NEW DAY YESTERDAY

Words and Music by
IAN ANDERSON

Verse:
w/Riff A1 (Gtr. 2, 4 times)
1. My first and last time with you
2. 3. See additional lyrics
and we had some fun.
Gtr. 1
Went walk - ing through the trees, yeah.
and then I kissed you once.
A
E
C
E
Oh,
I wan-na see you soon,
But I won-der how.
It was a
G
A
To Coda
C
new
day
yes - ter - day,
but it's an
old
day
now.

1.
w/Riff A1 (Gtr. 2, 2 times)
E5
1/4
2.
w/Riff A1 (Gtr. 2, 4 times)
E5
1/4
Guitar Solo:
Gtr. 2
N.C.(E5)
P.M.
Gtr. 1

8:6
w/Riffs A (Gtr. 1) & A1 (Gtr. 2), both 2 times
Flute Solo:
w/Riff A (Gtr. 1, 8 times)
D.S. % al Coda

Verses 2 & 3:
Spent a long time looking for a game to play.
My luck should be so bad now, to turn out this way.
I had to leave today, just when I thought I'd found you.
It was a new day yesterday, but it's an old day now.
(To Guitar Solo:)

TO CRY YOU A SONG

Words and Music by
IAN ANDERSON

(Cm)
F
C
how man - y cig - a - rettes did I bring a -
Gtr. 2
Gtrs. 1 & 2
Gtr. 1
w/Riffs A (Gtr. 1) & A1 (Gtr. 2), both 2 times
(Gm)
(B♭)
(Gm)
(B♭)
(Gm)
long.
G5
C5
When I get down I jump in a tax - i - cab,
Gtrs. 1 & 2
(Cm)
G5
C
F
C
driv - ing through Lon - don town to cry you a
Gtr. 2
Gtrs. 1 & 2
Gtr. 1
hold
hold

w/Riffs A (Gtr. 1) & A1 (Gtr. 2), both 2 times
w/Riffs B (Gtr. 1) & B1 (Gtr. 2)
(Gm) (B♭) (Gm) (B♭) (Gm)
song.
F C G5
It's been a
Gtrs. 1 & 2
Chorus:
C G5
long time, still shak - in' my wings. Well, I'm a
hold
C G5
glad bird, I got chang - es to ring.
hold

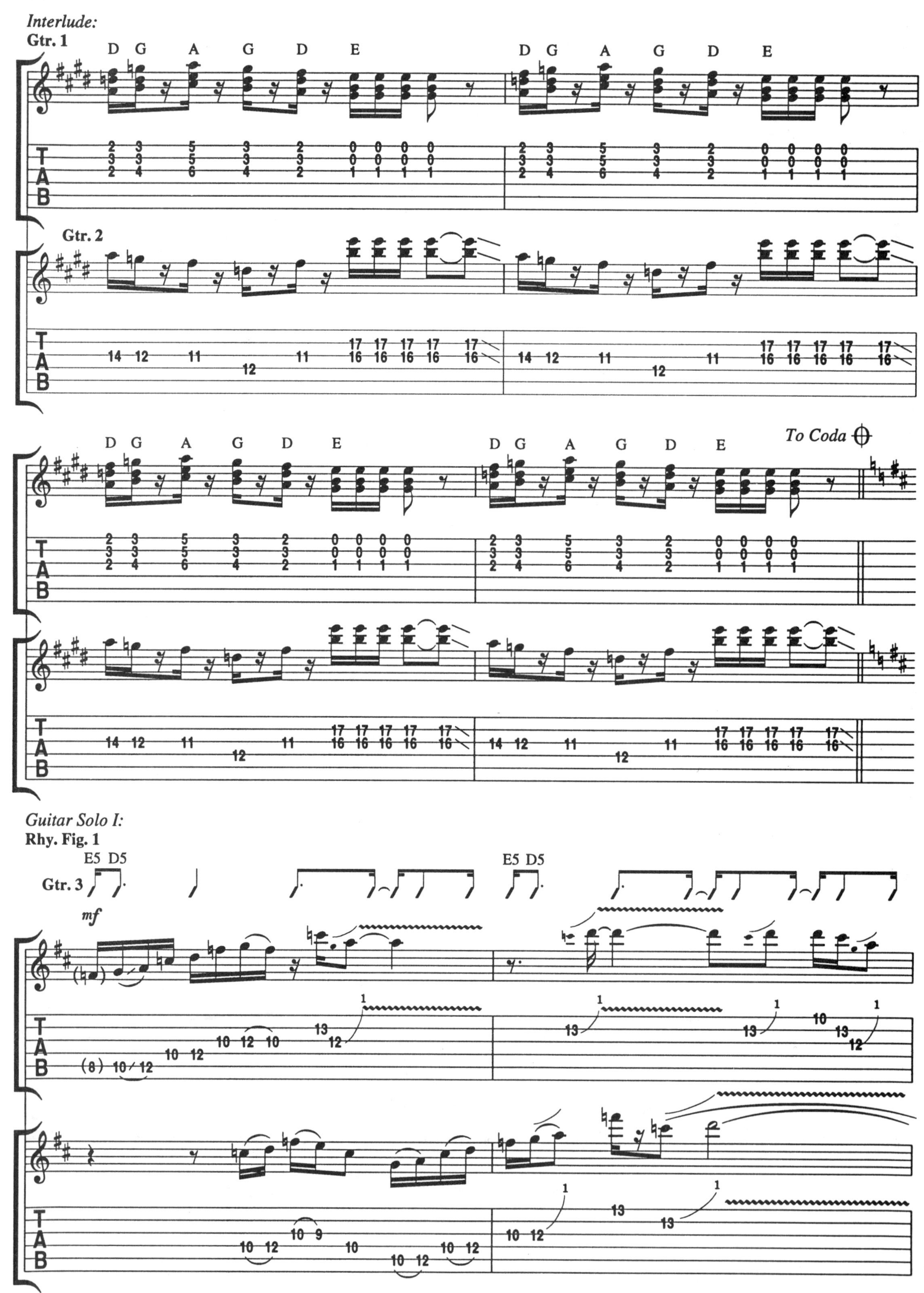
Interlude:
Gtr. 1
D G A G D E
D G A G D E
Gtr. 2
D G A G D E
D G A G D E
To Coda
Guitar Solo I:
Rhy. Fig. 1
E5 D5
Gtr. 3
mf
E5 D5

④ open
E5 D5
D
D C
④ open
D
G
F
1
1/2
1
1
1
(end Rhy. Fig. 1)
C5
B♭5
F5 G5
G
F
C5
B♭5
F5 G5
1-1/2
* N.C. (Dm)
Rhy. Fig. 2
1

*Gtr. 3 tacet

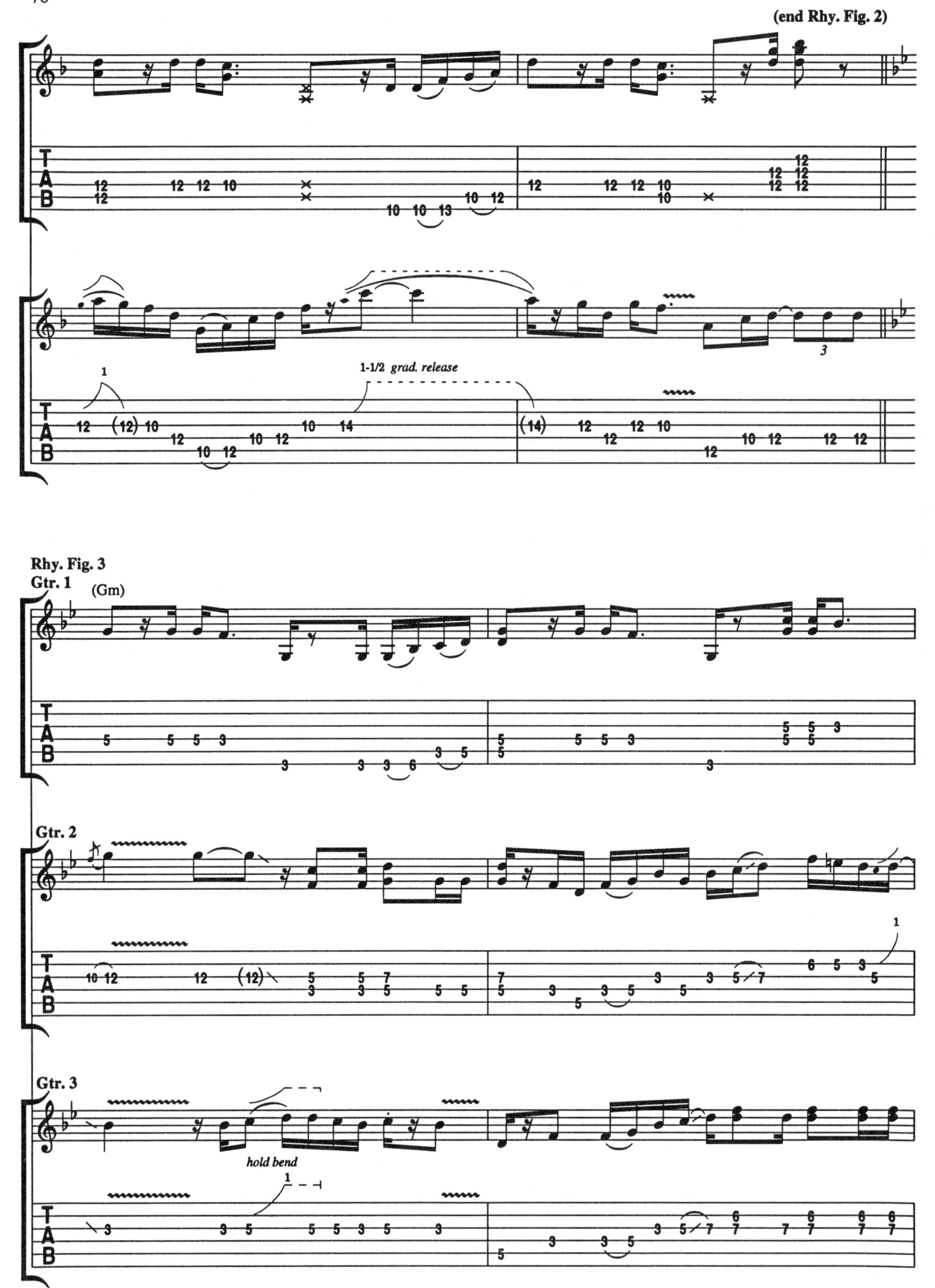
(end Rhy. Fig. 2)
1
1-1/2 grad. release
3
Rhy. Fig. 3
Gtr. 1
(Gm)
Gtr. 2
1
Gtr. 3
hold bend
1

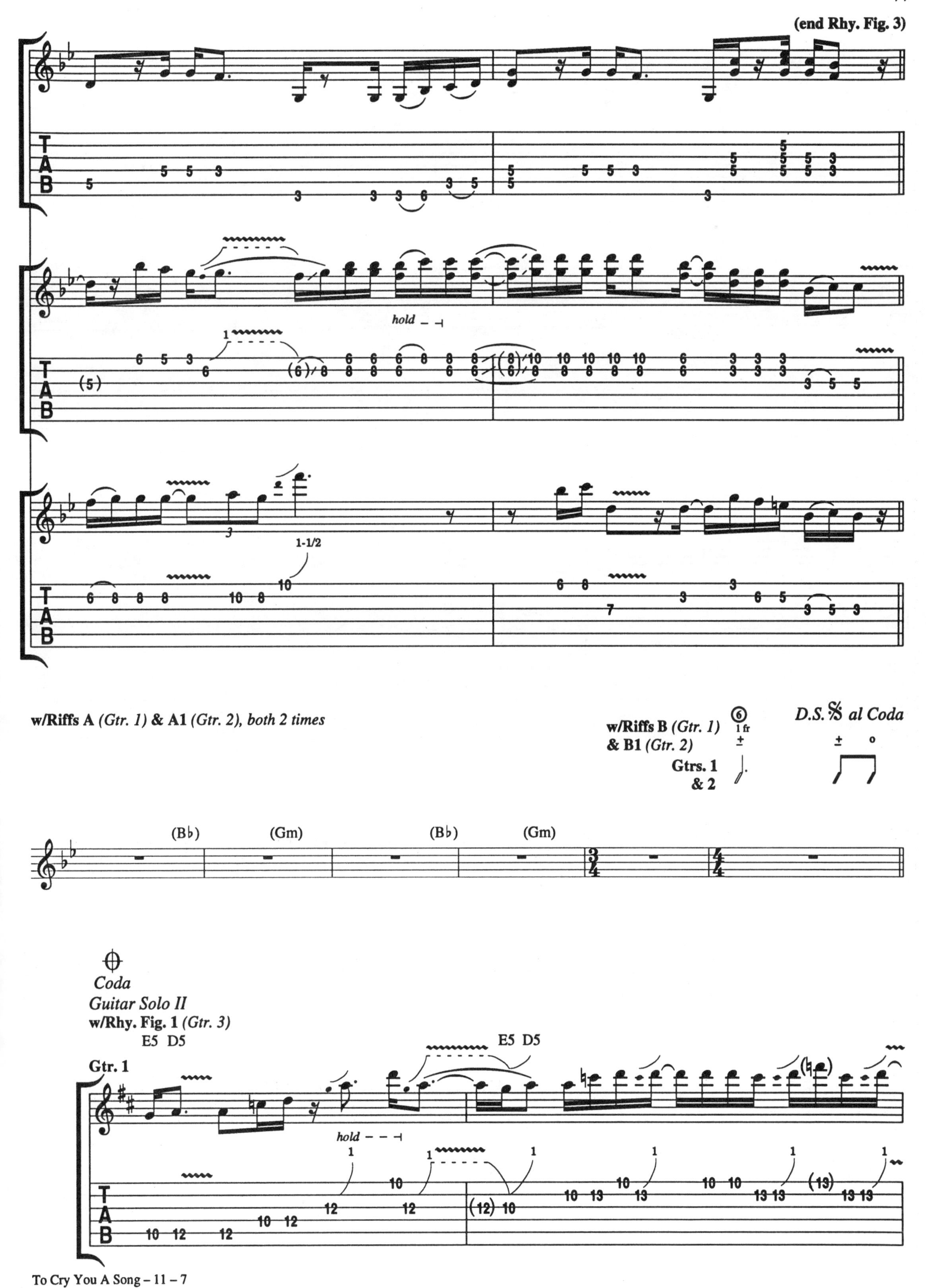
(end Rhy. Fig. 3)
hold
1-1/2
w/Riffs A (Gtr. 1) & A1 (Gtr. 2), both 2 times
w/Riffs B (Gtr. 1)
& B1 (Gtr. 2)
Gtrs. 1
& 2
1 fr
D.S. al Coda
(B♭)
(Gm)
(B♭)
(Gm)
Coda
Guitar Solo II
w/Rhy. Fig. 1 (Gtr. 3)
E5 D5
E5 D5
Gtr. 1
hold

E5
D5
C
G
F
Gtr. 2
C5 B♭5
F5
G5
G
F
grad. release
C5
B♭5
F5
G5
w/Rhy. Fig. 2 (Gtr. 1)
Gtr. 2
*(Dm)
*Gtr. 3 tacet

*Gtr. 4 played through Leslie speaker cabinet.

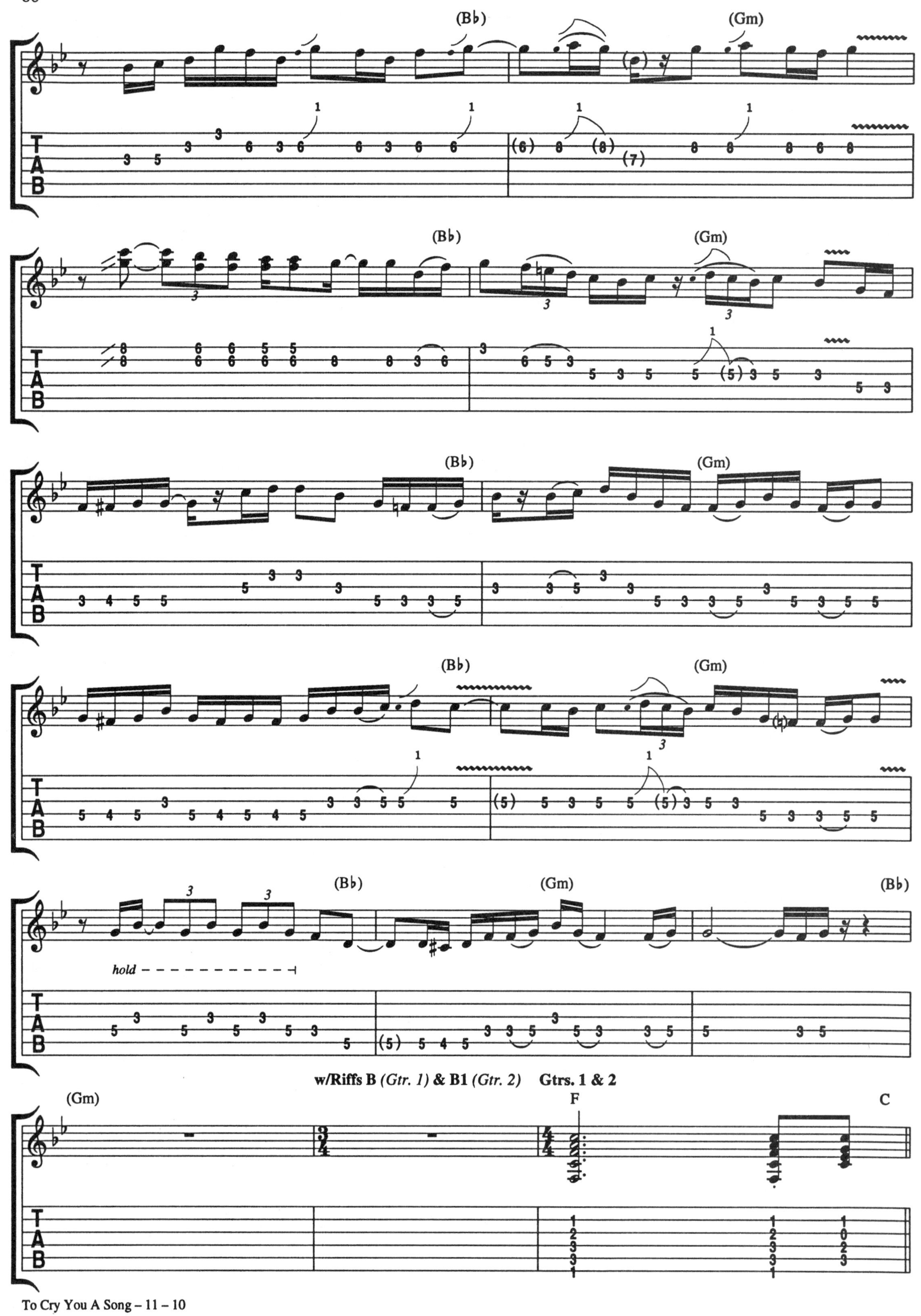
(B♭)
(Gm)
(B♭)
(Gm)
(B♭)
(Gm)
(B♭)
(Gm)
(B♭)
(Gm)
(B♭)
hold
(Gm)
w/Riffs B (Gtr. 1) & B1 (Gtr. 2)
Gtrs. 1 & 2
F
C

*2 Gtrs. arr. for 1.

Verse 2:
Closing my dream inside this paperback,
Thought I saw angels but I could have been wrong.
Search in my case, can't find what they're looking for,
Waving me through to cry you a song.
(To Bridge:)

Verse 4:
The smile in your eyes was never so sweet before,
I came down from the skies to cry you a song.

NOTHING IS EASY

Words and Music by
IAN ANDERSON

w/Fill 1 (Gtr. 2)
B♭
Gm
friend it's o - kay.
Just
(end Rhy. Fig. 1)
w/Rhy. Fig. 1 (Gtr. 1, 3 times)
Dm
C
F
C
B♭
w/Fill 1 (Gtr. 2)
Gm
take your life eas - y and stop all that hur-ry'ing, be hap - py my way.

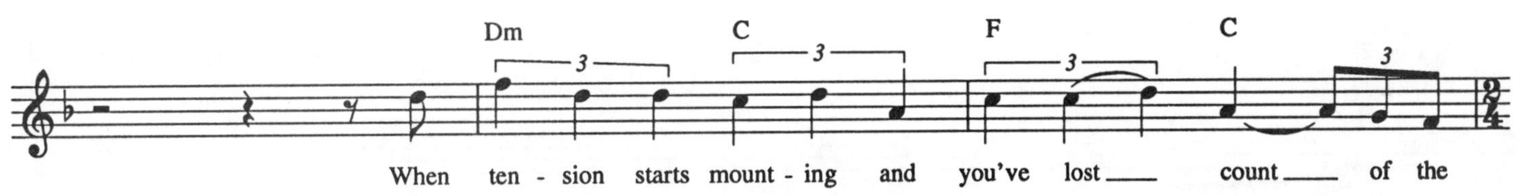

Dm
C
F
C
When ten - sion starts mount - ing and you've lost count of the

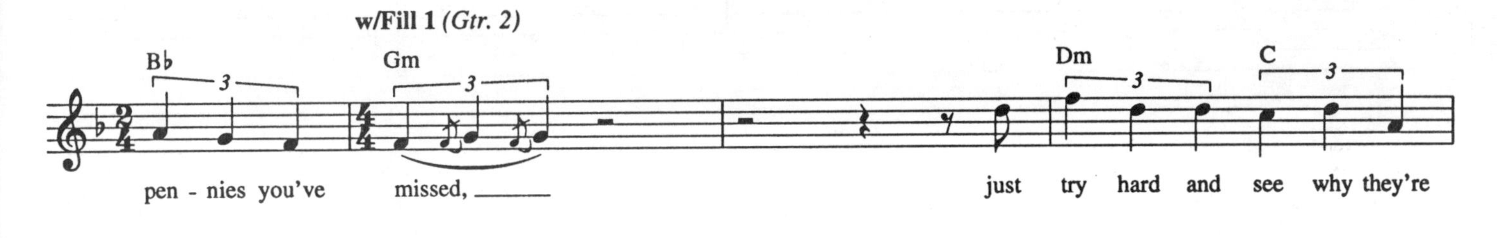

w/Fill 1 (Gtr. 2)
B♭
Gm
Dm
C
pen - nies you've missed,
just try hard and see why they're

w/Fill 1 (Gtr. 2)
F
C
B♭
Gm
not wor-ry'ng me, the're last on my list.
Noth-ing's

Fill 1
Gtr. 2

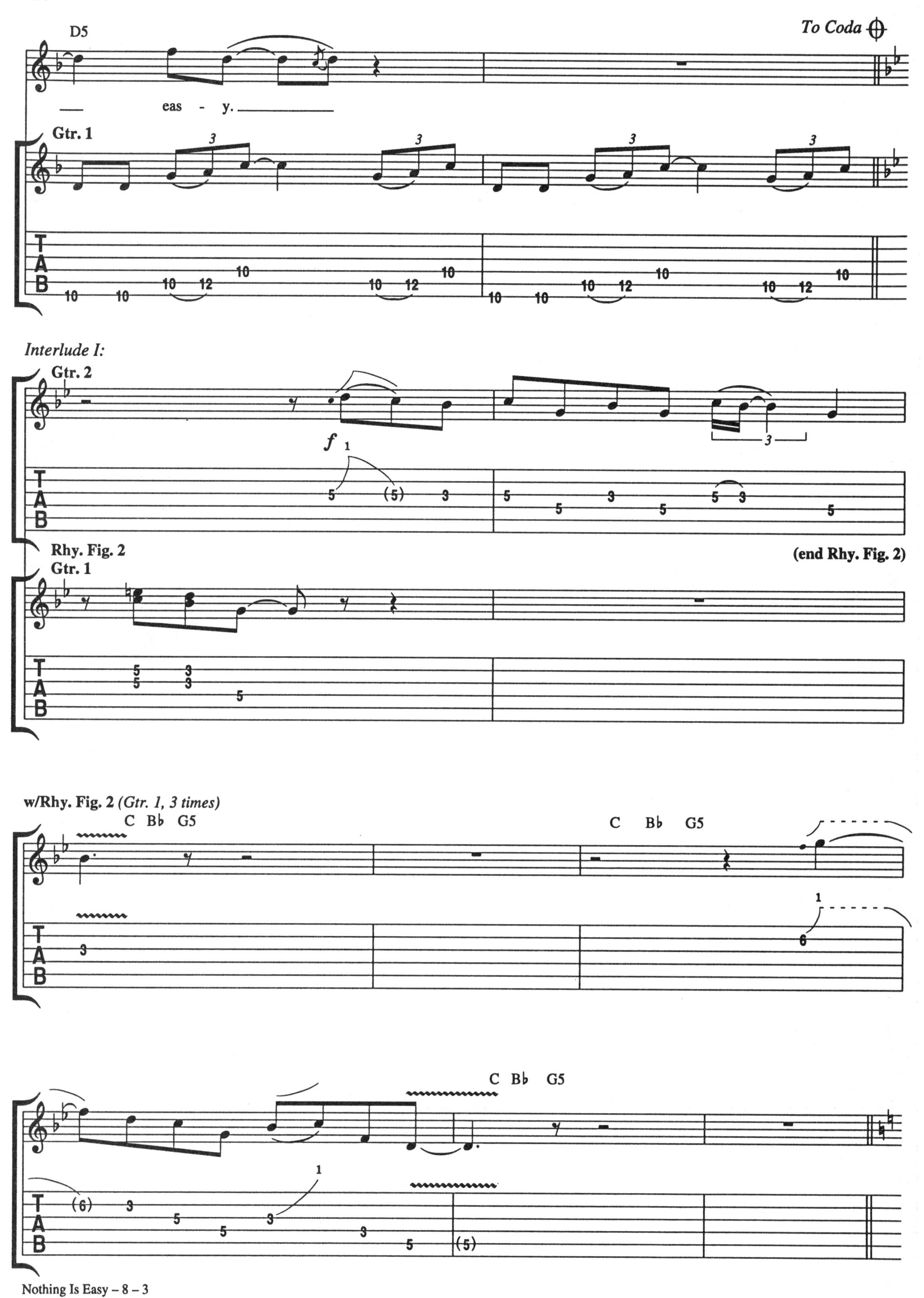
D5
To Coda
eas - y.
Gtr. 1
Interlude I:
Gtr. 2
Rhy. Fig. 2
Gtr. 1
(end Rhy. Fig. 2)
w/Rhy. Fig. 2 (Gtr. 1, 3 times)
C Bb G5
C Bb G5
C Bb G5

*Bass gtr. plays G.

w/Rhy. Fig. 4 (Gtr. 1, 3 times)
Flute Solo:
Am D7 G6 D7 Am D7 G6 D7 Am D7 G6 D7
D.C. 𝄋 al Coda
Rhy. Fig. 5
Gtr. 1
D C A5
(end Rhy. Fig. 5)
Interlude II:
w/Rhy. Fig. 2 (Gtr. 1, 4 times)
Coda
C B♭ G5
Gtr. 2
Guitar Solo II:
w/Rhy. Fig. 3 (Gtr. 1, 2 times)
N.C.(A5)
hold
w/Rhy. Fig. 5 (Gtr. 1)
1/4

Outro:
(Drum fill)
D C A5
D C A5
Am7
Gtr. 1
1/4
3
D C A5
D C A5
Am7 (Bass Gtr. fill)
(Drum fill)
D C A5
D C A5
Am7
Gtr. 2
straight ♪'s
Gtr. 1

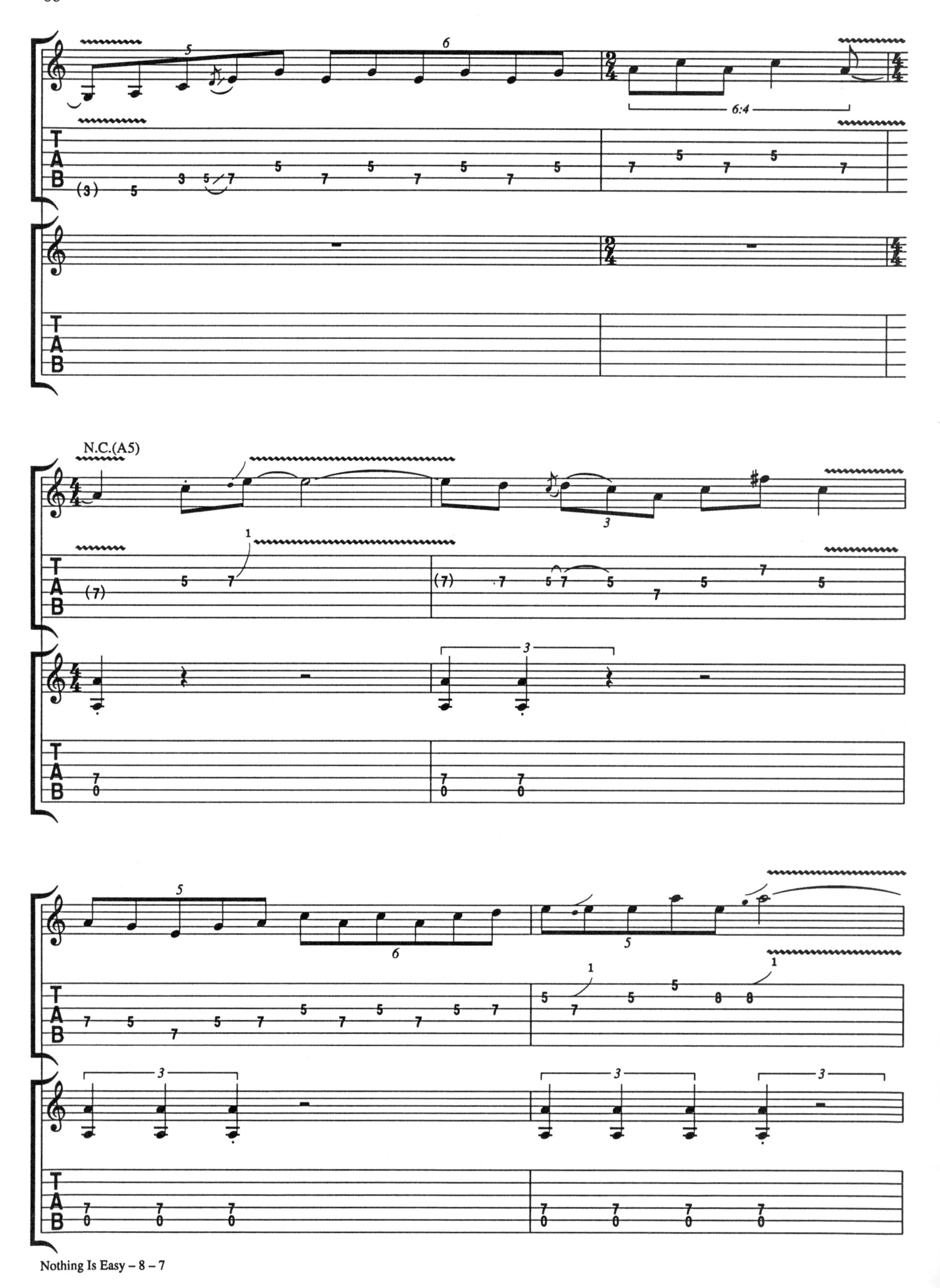
N.C.(A5)

Verse 2:

Nothing is easy you'll find that
The squeeze won't turn out so bad.
Your fingers may freeze, worse things
Happen at sea, there's good times to be had.
So if you're alone and you're down to the bone
Just give us a play.
You'll smile in a while and discover that
I'll get you happy my way.
Nothing's easy.

(To Interlude II:)

SKATING AWAY (ON THE THIN ICE OF THE NEW DAY)

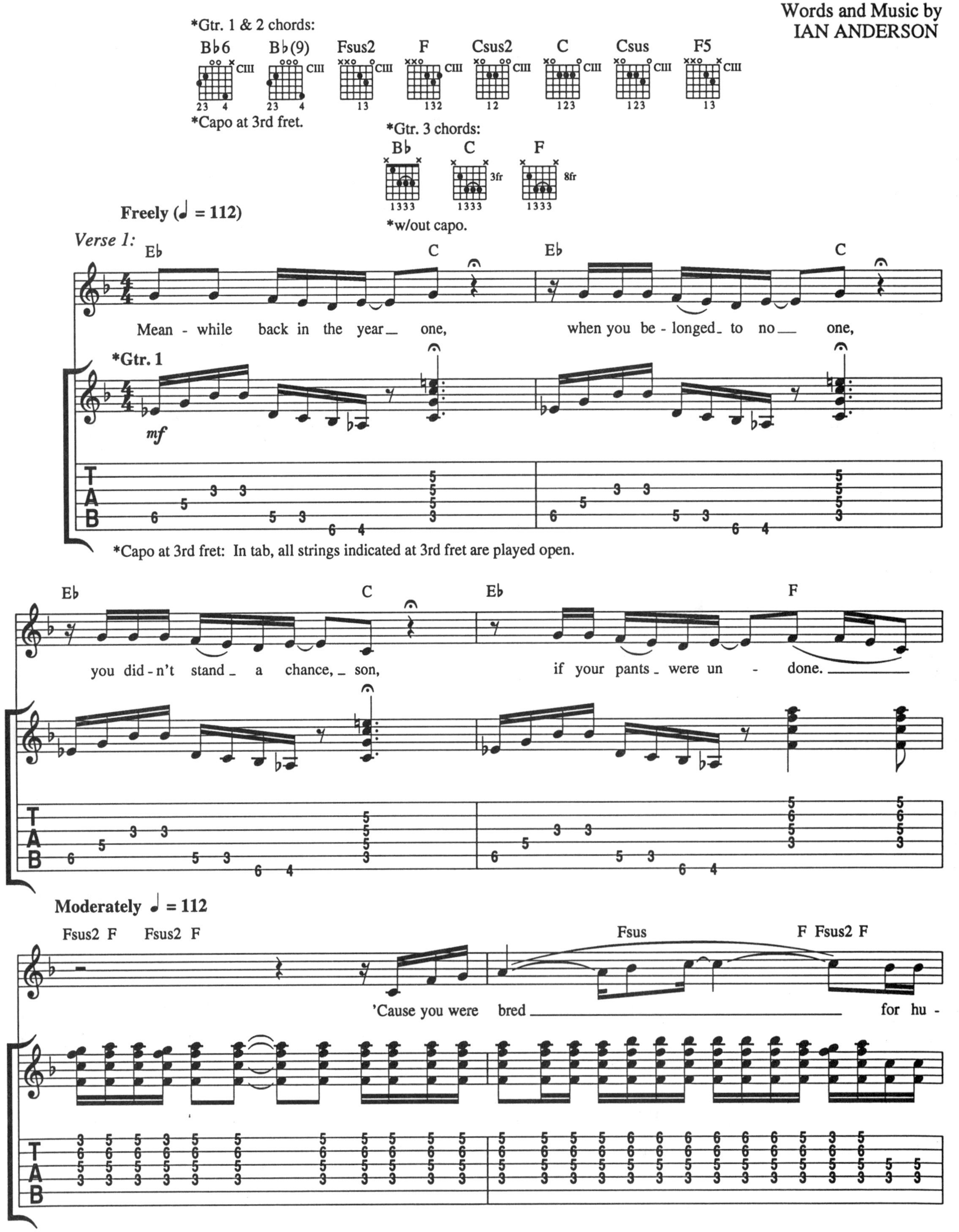

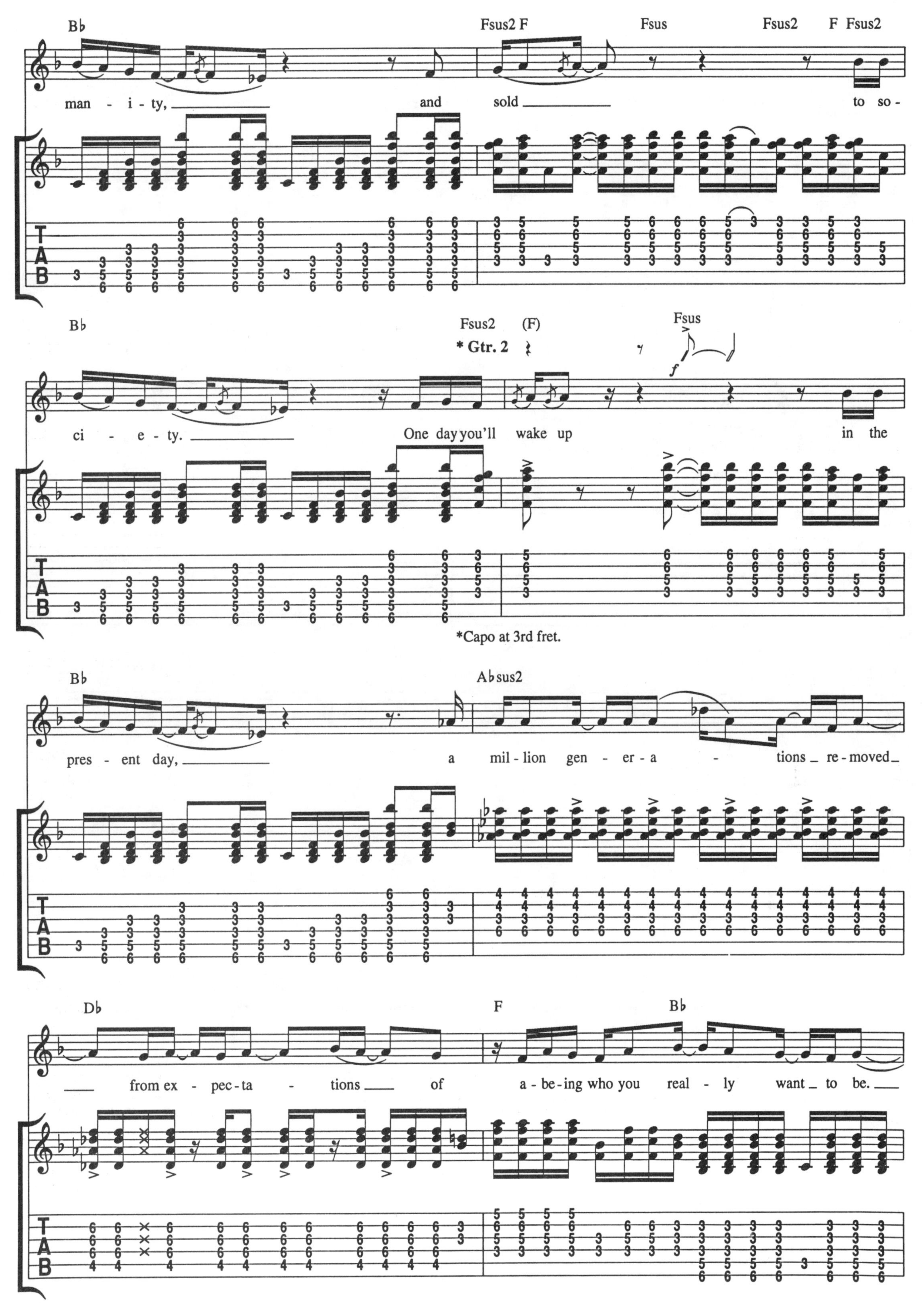

B♭
Fsus2 F
Fsus
Fsus2
F Fsus2
man - i - ty,
and
sold
to so -
B♭
Fsus2
(F)
* Gtr. 2
Fsus
ci - e - ty.
One day you'll
wake up
in the
*Capo at 3rd fret.
B♭
A♭sus2
pres - ent day,
a
mil - lion
gen - er - a - tions re - moved
D♭
F
B♭
from ex - pec - ta - tions
of
a - be - ing who you
real - ly
want to
be.

Chorus:
w/Rhy. Fill 1 (Gtr. 2, 3 times)
C Csus2 C Csus Csus2 C (B♭5) F
Skat-ing a-way,
skat-ing a-way,
Rhy. Fig. 1
skat-ing a-way
on the thin ice
of the new day,
E♭
B♭
Fsus F Fsus F Fsus2 F
ay.
(end Rhy. Fig. 1)

Rhy. Fill 1
Gtr. 2
hold

Verses 2 & 3:

Rhy. Fig. 2
Gtr. 1
B♭6 B♭(9)
Fsus2 F
Fsus F
Fsus2
2. So as you push off from the shore, a-won't you turn your head once more,
3. See additional lyrics.
(end Rhy. Fig. 2)
Csus C Csus2 C Csus
C Csus2 F
Fsus F F5
B♭6
and make your peace with ev - 'ry - one?
w/Rhy. Fig. 2 (Gtr. 1)
B♭6 B♭(9)
Fsus2 F
Fsus F Fsus2
For those who choose to stay a - will live just one more day
Csus2 C Csus2 C Csus
C Csus2
F
Fsus2 F F5
B♭6
to do the things they should have done.
*Gtr. 3 (Electric)
B♭
C
And as you cross the wil - der - ness, a - spin - ning in your emp - ti-ness, you feel you have
Gtr. 2
* Gtr. 3 is not capoed.
F
Fsus F F5 Fsus F Fsus2 Fsus
to pray.
* Next 2 bars 2 gtrs arr. for 1

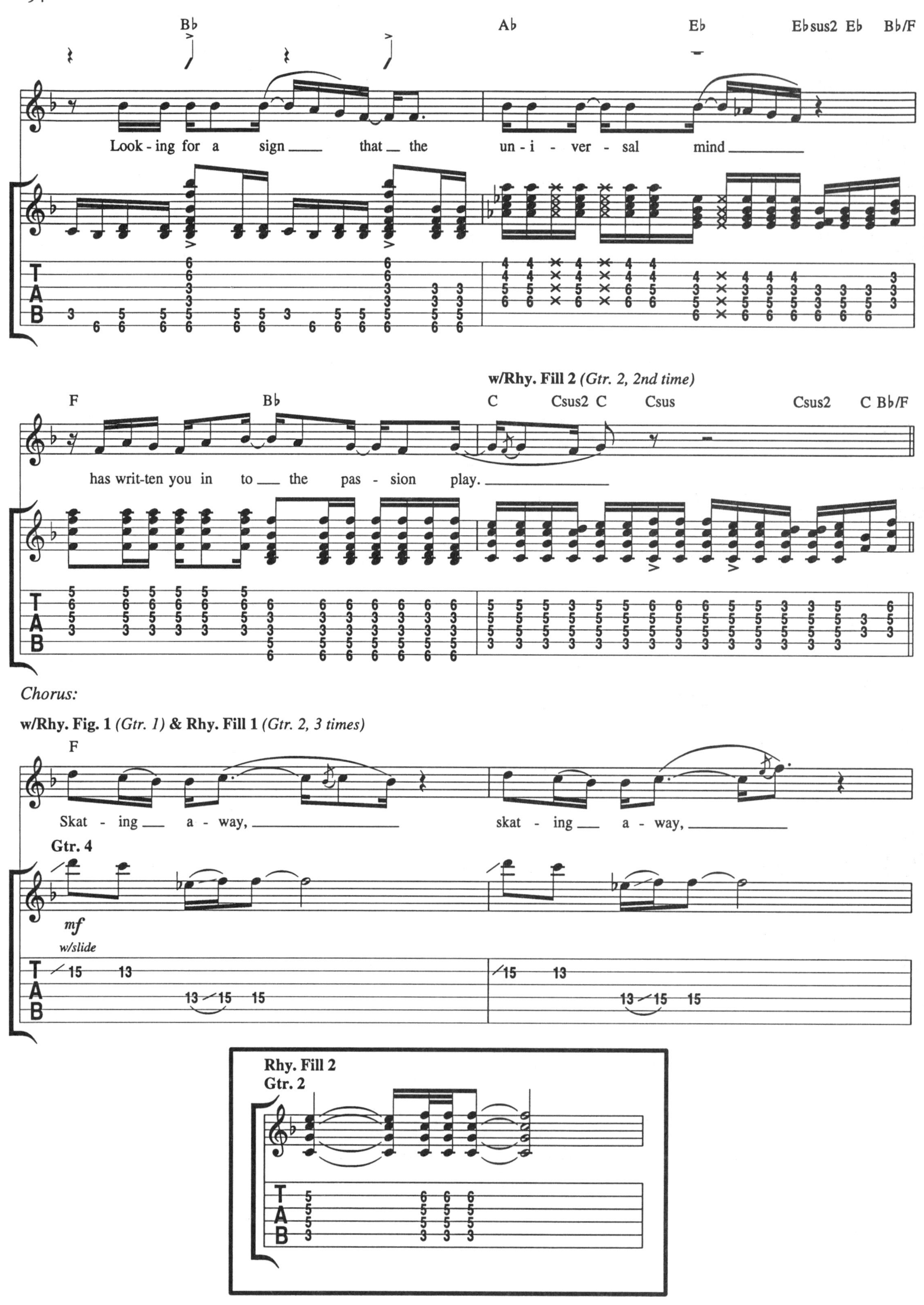
Bb
Ab
Eb
Ebsus2 Eb
Bb/F
Look - ing for a sign ___ that ___ the un - i - ver - sal mind ___
w/Rhy. Fill 2 (Gtr. 2, 2nd time)
F
Bb
C
Csus2 C
Csus
Csus2
C Bb/F
has writ-ten you in to ___ the pas - sion play. ___
Chorus:
w/Rhy. Fig. 1 (Gtr. 1) & Rhy. Fill 1 (Gtr. 2, 3 times)
F
Skat - ing ___ a - way, ___
skat - ing ___ a - way, ___
Gtr. 4
mf
w/slide
Rhy. Fill 2
Gtr. 2

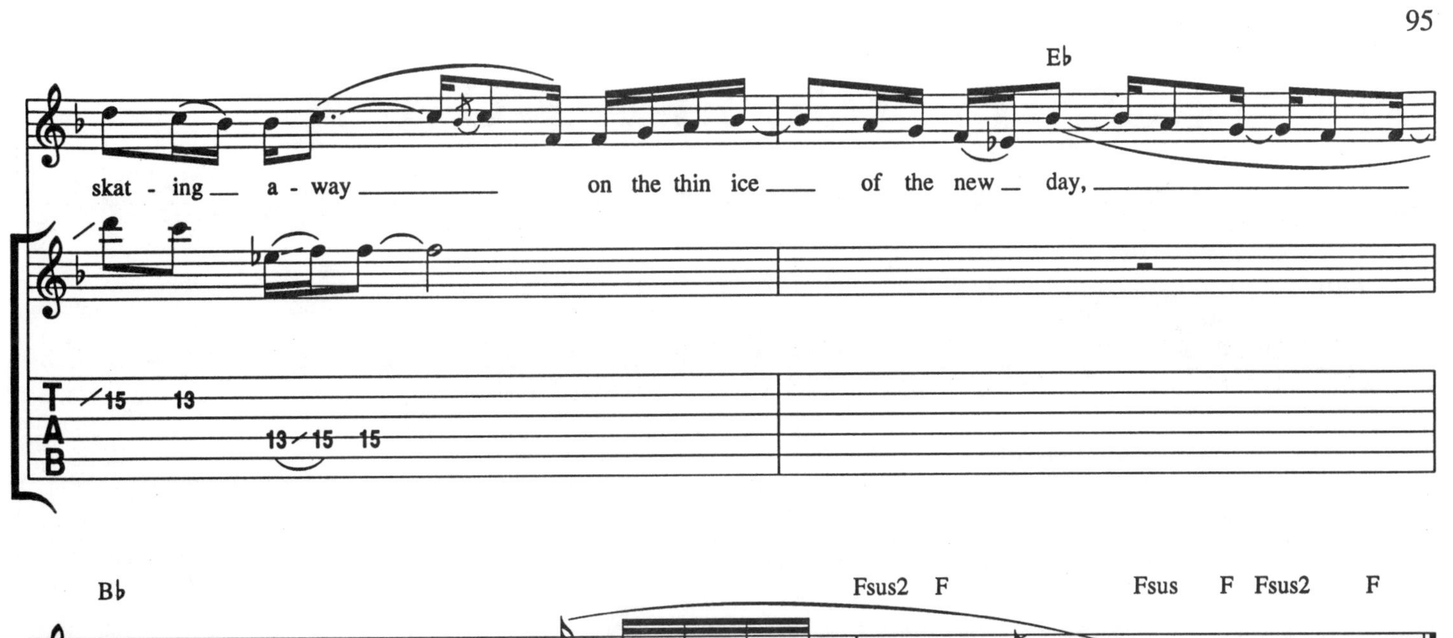

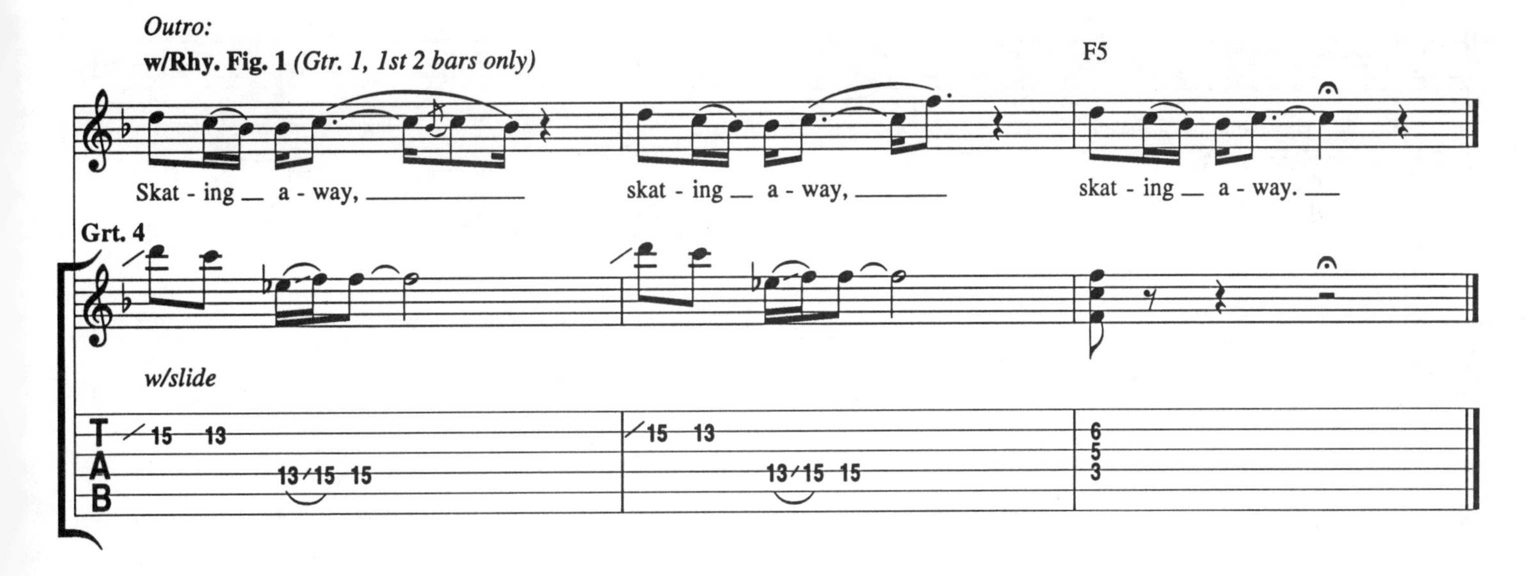

Verse 3:
And as you cross the circle line,
Well, the ice wall creaks behind;
You're a rabbit on the run.
And silver splinters fly in the corner of your eye,
Shining in the setting sun.
Well, do you ever get the feeling that the
Story's too damn real and in the present tense?
Or that everybody's on the stage and it seems
Like you're the only person sitting in the audience?
(To Chorus:)

SOSSITY, YOU'RE A WOMAN

Words and Music by
IAN ANDERSON

F/C
C5 A5
Am7
Am
hope ___ we can't see where _ you've been.
The smil - ing face _
C
G
(Am)
C A5
C
E
(Em)
___ that you've worn ______
to greet _ me ris - ing at morn - ing. _
Cm/G
B♭
Sent me out _____ to work _ for ___ my score. ________
To Coda
A5
Am
C
G/B
Please me ______ and say what it's for. ________
T
A
B

Chorus:
A5
G/A
Am
A5
Am7(#5)
Sos - si - ty
you're a
D5
Em7
Am
wom - an.
A5
G/A
D/A G/A Am
Am7(#5)
So - ci - e - ty
you're a
D5
Em7
A5
wom - an.
D.C. al Coda I
To Coda II

Verse 2:
Give me the straight-laced promise
And not the pathetic lie.
Tie me down with your ribbons,
And sulk when I ask you why.
Your Sunday-paper voice cries
Demanding truths I deny.
The bitter-sweet kiss you pretended
Is offered, our affair mended.
(To Chorus:)

Verse 3:
All of the tears you're wasting
Are for yourself and not for me.
It's sad to know you're aging,
Sadder still to admit I'm free.
Your immature physical toy
Has grown too young to enjoy.
At last your straight-laced agreement
Woman, you were too old for me.
(To Chorus:)

TEACHER

Words and music by
IAN ANDERSON

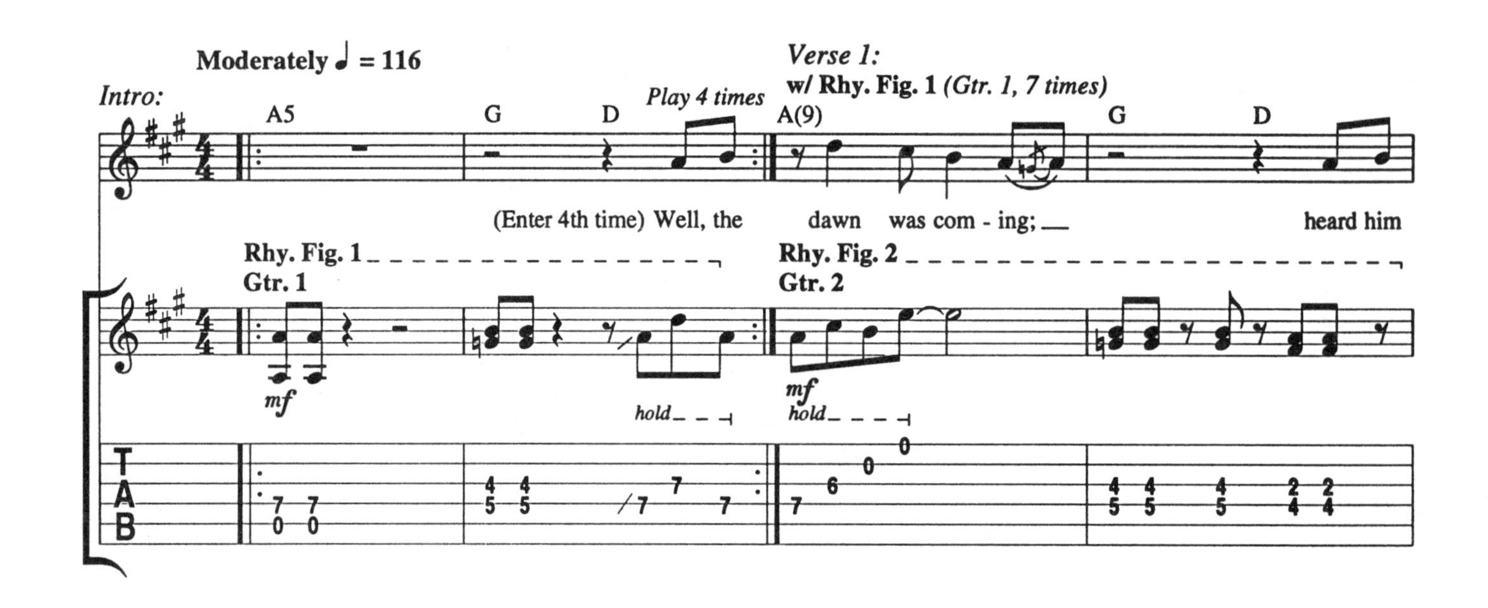

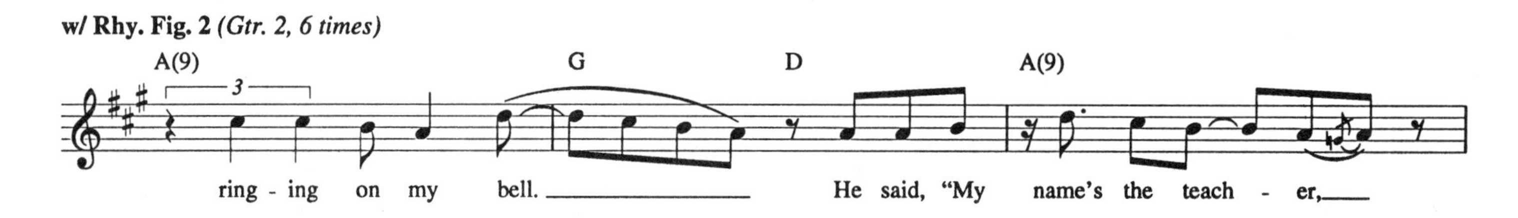

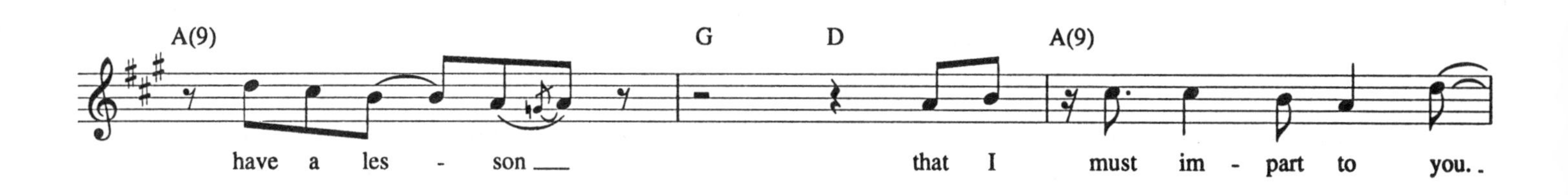

w/ Rhy. Fig. 3A (Gtr. 2)
Pre- Chorus:
A(9)
G
A
C
D
must in - sist it's true.
Jump up, look a - round, find
Rhy. Fig. 3
Gtr. 1
Rhy. Fig. 4
Gtr. 1 & 2
hold
F
D
C
your - self some fun,
no sense in sit-ting there hat - ing ev' - ry one.
hold
No man's an is - land and his cas-tle is-n't home, the nest is full of noth-ing when the bird has
(end Rhy. Fig. 4)

Fill 1
Gtr. 2
Rhy. Fig. 3A
hold

*Interlude:
N.C. (B5)
(E5)
(A5)
(B5)
(E5)
(A5)
(B5)
flown.
Riff A
Gtr. 1
Riff A1
Gtr. 2
* w/ out vocal on repeat
(E5)
(A5)
(B5)
(E5)
(A5)
2. So,
3. See additional lyrics.
(end Riff A)
(end Riff A1)

Verses 2 & 3:
w/ Rhy. Figs. 1 (Gtr. 1) & 2 (Gtr. 2), both 3 times
A(9)
G
D
A(9)
I took a jour - ney,
threw my world in - to the sea.
G
D
A(9)
G
D
With me went the teach - er
who found
w/ Rhy. Figs. 3 (Gtr. 1) & 3A (Gtr. 2)
A(9)
G
A
C
fun in - stead of me.
Pre-chorus:
w/ Rhy. Fig. 4 (Gtrs. 1 & 2)
D
Hey man, what's the plan, what
F
D
C
was that you said?
D
Sun tanned, drink in hand, ly - ing there in bed.
F
D
C
D
I try to so - cia-lize, but
F
D
C
I can't seem to find
D
what I was look-ing for, got
Interlude:
To Coda
w/ Riffs A (Gtr. 1) & A1 (Gtr. 2)
F
some-thing on my
N.C. (B5)
(E5)
(A5)
(B5)
(E5)
mind.
(A5)
(B5)
(E5)
(A5)
(B5)
(E5)
(A5)
Flute Solo:
Rhy. Fig. 5
Gtr. 1
A5
C5
D5
C5
A5
G5
A5
G5 A5
C5

Double time
D5
C5
A5
N.C. (A5)
8va
Fdbk.
(end Rhy. Fig. 5)

Verse 3:

Then the teacher told me it had been a lot of fun.
Thanked me for his ticket and all that I had done.

(To Pre-Chorus:)

TOO OLD TO ROCK 'N' ROLL: TOO YOUNG TO DIE

Words and Music by
IAN ANDERSON

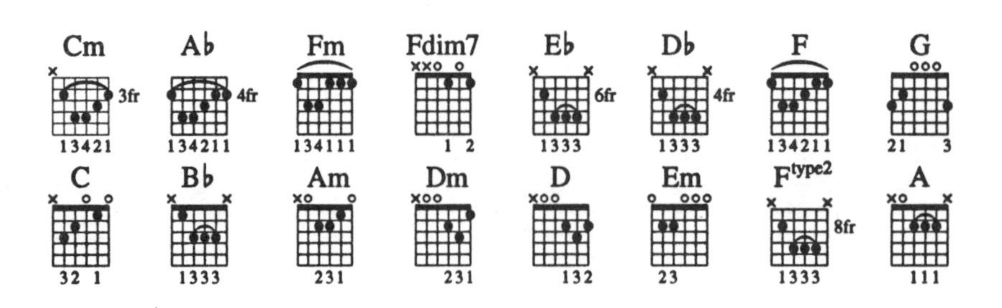

Moderately slow ♩ = 72

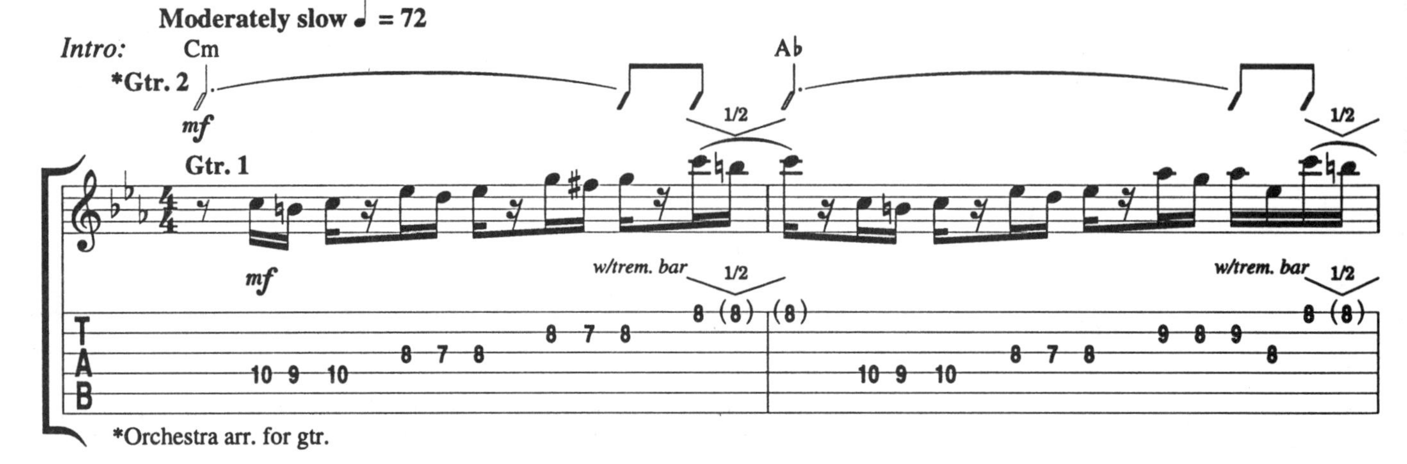

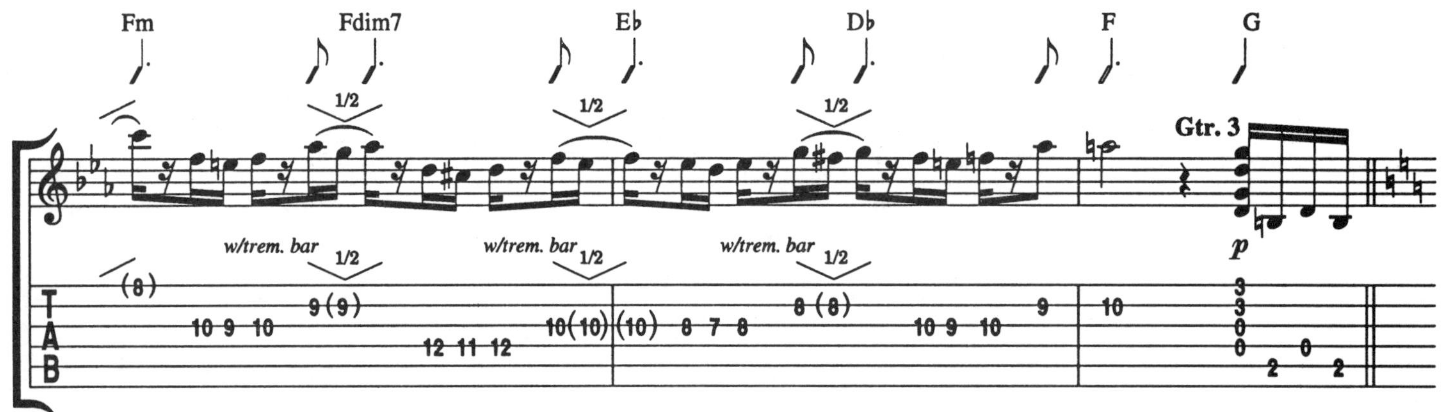

Am
Dm
G
wore his trou - ser cuffs _ too ___ tight.
hold
hold
hold
C
F
C
G
C
B♭
Un-fash-ion - a - ble to ___ the end, ___
Am
Dm
G
(end Rhy. Fig. 1)
drank ___ his ale too ___ light.
(end Rhy. Fig. 1A)
hold
hold

Verses 2 & 7:
Rhy. Fig. 2
C G D G F
2. Death's head belt buck - le, yes - ter - day's dreams,
7. See additional lyrics.
Rhy. Fig. 2A
Em Am D
the trans - port caf' proph - et of doom.
G C G D G F
Ring - ing no change in his doub - le sewn seams, in his
Rhy. Fig. 2A

To Coda
(end Rhy. Fig. 2)
Em
Am
D
E♭
Ftype2
post war ba - by gloom.
Now he's
And he was
(end Rhy. Fig. 2A)
Chorus:
Rhy. Fig. 3
B♭
C
B♭
F
B♭
F
too old to rock 'n' roll,
Rhy. Fig. 3A
E♭
A
Dm
E♭
Ftype2
but he's too young to die.
Yes, he's

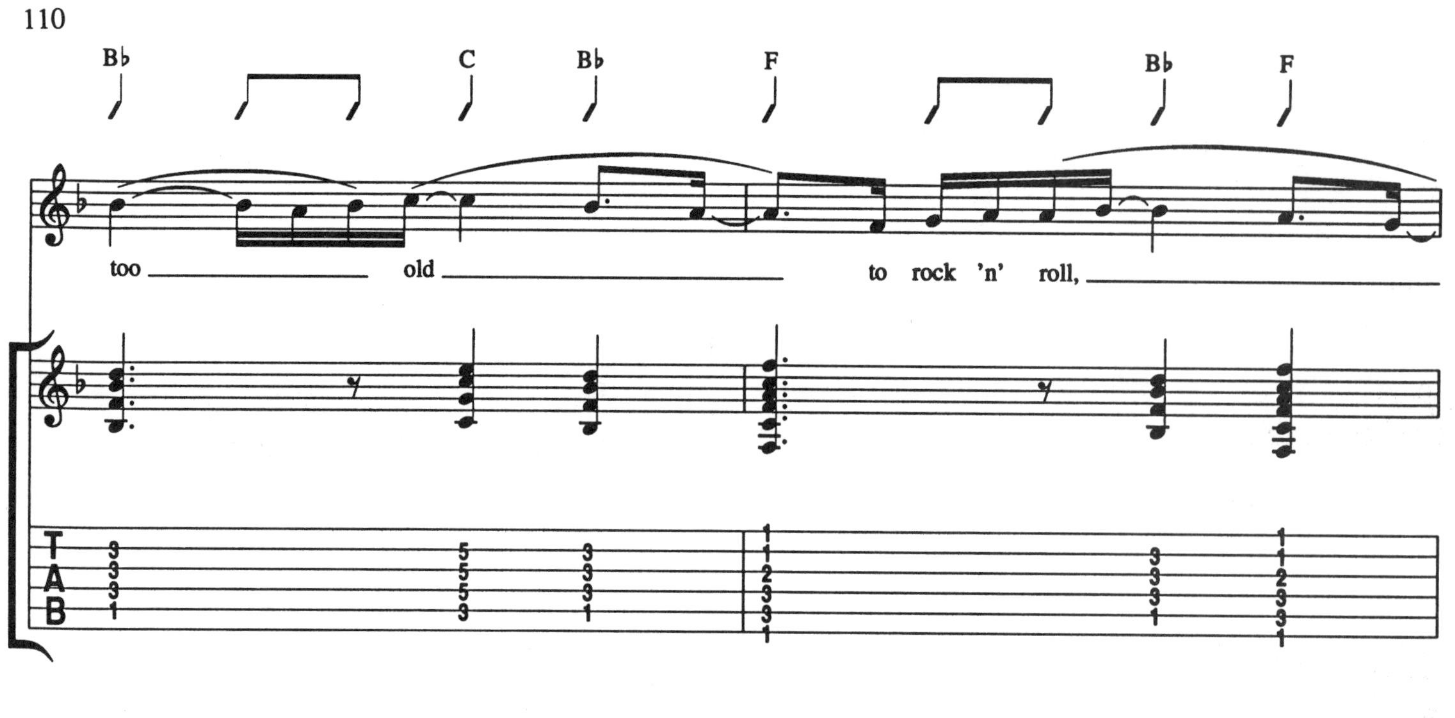

B♭ C B♭ F B♭ F
too old to rock 'n' roll,

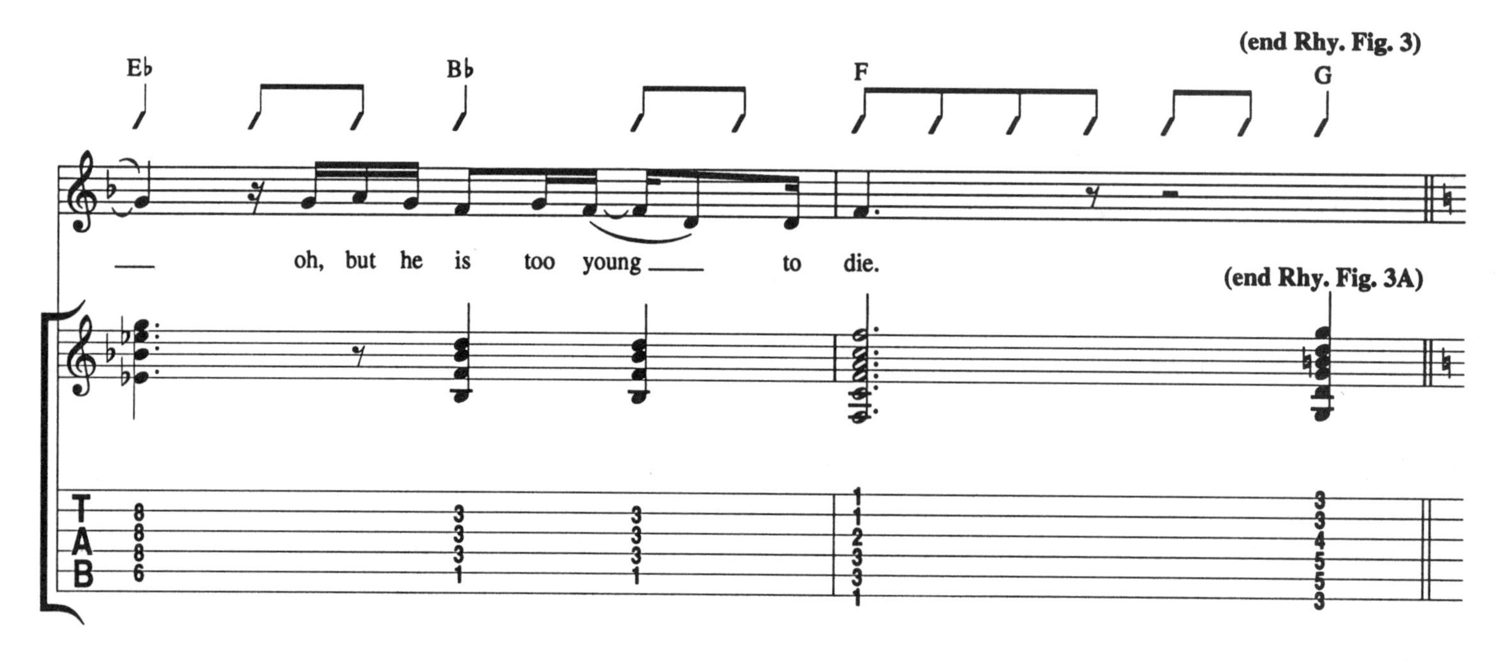

(end Rhy. Fig. 3)
E♭ B♭ F G
oh, but he is too young to die.
(end Rhy. Fig. 3A)

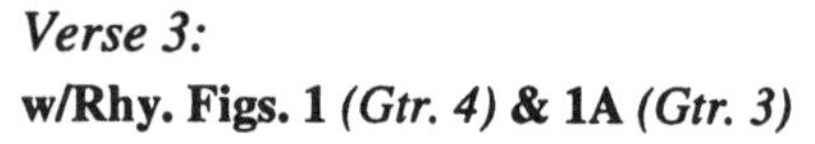

Verse 3:
w/Rhy. Figs. 1 (Gtr. 4) & 1A (Gtr. 3)

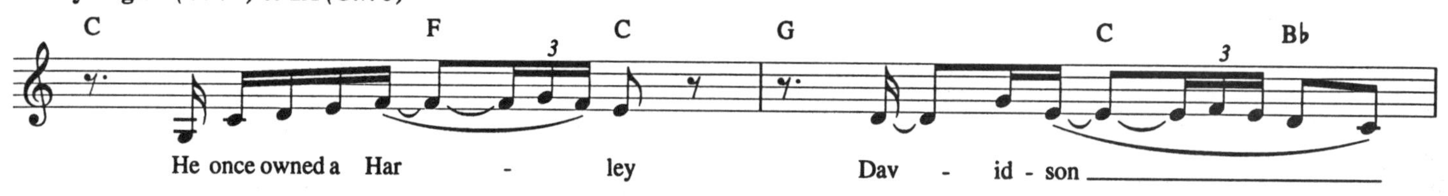

C F C G C B♭
He once owned a Har - ley Dav - id - son

Am Dm G C F C
and a Tri - umph Bon - ne - ville. Count - ed his friends in

G C Bb Am Dm G
burnt - out spark plugs, and prays that he al - ways will.
Verse 4:
w/Rhy. Figs. 2 (Gtr. 4) & 2A (Gtr. 3), 1st 4 bars only, both 2 times.
C G D G F
But he's the last of the blue - bloods, a greas - er boy,
Em Am D G C G
and all his mates are do - ing time. Mar-ried with three kids
D G F Em Am D
up by the ring road, sold their souls straight down the line.
Verse 5:
w/Rhy. Figs. 2 (Gtr. 4) & 2A (Gtr. 3)
G C G D G F
And some of them own oh, lit - tle sports cars,
Em Am D
and meet at the ten - nis club do's
G C G D G F
for drinks on a Sun - day, work on Mon - day.
Em Am D Eb F
They've thrown a - way their blue suede shoes. Now they're

Chorus:
w/Rhy. Figs. 3 (Gtr. 4) & 3A (Gtr. 3)
Bb C Bb F Bb F
too old to rock 'n' roll
Riff A
Gtr. 1
Eb A Dm Eb F
and they're too young to die. Yes, they're
Bb C Bb F Bb F
too old to rock 'n' roll
D.C. al Coda
Eb Bb F G
and they're too young to die.
(end Riff A)

Coda
w/Rhy. Figs. 3 (Gtr. 4) & 3A (Gtr. 3), 1st 7 bars only, & w/Riff A (Gtr. 1)
B♭ C B♭ F B♭ F
too old to rock 'n' roll
E♭ A Dm E♭ F type2
and he was too young to die. Oh, he was
B♭ C B♭ F B♭ F
too old to rock 'n' roll
w/Rhy. Fills 1 (Gtr. 4) & 1A (Gtr. 3)
E♭ B♭ F
and he was too young to die. Now you're
Double Time (♩ = 144)
B♭ C F
Gtr. 3
(Cont. rhy. simile)
ah, nev - er too old to rock 'n' roll,
Gtr. 1
Rhy. Fill 1
F
Gtr. 4
Rhy. Fill 1A
Gtr. 3

B♭
F
E♭
B♭
if you're too young to die.
F
And now you're
B♭
C
F
ah, nev - er too old
to rock 'n' roll,
Freely
B♭
F
E♭
B♭
But he was too young to
T
A
B

Verse 6:
So the old rocker gets out his bike
To make a ton before he takes his leave.
Up on the A1, by Scotch Corner,
Just like it used to be.

Verse 7:
And as he flies, tears in his eyes,
His wind-whipped words echo the final take.
As he hits the trunk road, doing around one-hundred twenty,
With no room left to brake.

THICK AS A BRICK

Words and Music by
IAN ANDERSON
and GERALD BOSTOCK

w/Rhy. Fig. 2 (Gtr. 1)
w/Rhy. Riff 1 (Gtr. 2, 2 times, Verse 2)
B♭
F5
C(4)
B♭
* Flute
- ness a ___ shout.
Gtr. 2 (Electric)
f
Verse 1 only
T
A
B
* Verse 1 only
w/Rhy. Fig. 1 (Gtr. 1)
Fsus
E♭sus2
B♭
F
I may make you feel, ___
Rhy. Riff 1
(end Rhy. Riff 1)
hold
hold
hold
w/Rhy. Fig. 2 (Gtr. 1) & Rhy. Riff 1
(Gtr. 2, 2 times, Verse 2)
Cm
B♭
F5
C(4)
* Flute
___ but I can't make you think. ___
* Verse 1 only
B♭
Fsus
E♭sus2
B♭
your
w/Rhy. Fig. 1 (Gtr. 1)
F
Cm
B♭
sperm's in the gut - ter, your love's in the sink. ___
w/Rhy. Fig. 2 (Gtr. 1) & Rhy. Riff 1 (Gtr. 2, 2 times, Verse 2)
F5
C(4)
B♭
Fsus
E♭sus2
B♭
*Flute
1. So you
* Verse 1 only

Chorus:

Bb
C
Csus2
F
Fsus2
F
Fsus2
Gtr. 1
ride your - selves o - ver the fields,
2. See additional lyrics
Gtr. 2
Next 16 bars Chorus 2 only
T
A
B
F Fsus F Fsus2 Bb C Csus2
and you make all your an - i - mal deals,
F Fsus2 F Fsus2 F Fsus Fsus2 Bb C Csus2
and your wise men don't know how it feels
F Fsus2 F Fsus2 F Fsus Fsus2 C Csus C Csus2 C Csus C

w/Rhy. Fig. 2 (Gtr. 1, 2 times)
Csus2 C
F5 C(4)
Flute
to be thick as a brick.
Bb
Fsus Ebsus2
Bb
1.
w/Rhy. Riff 1 (Both gtrs, 2 times)
F Eb6 Bb F Eb6 Bb
2. And the
2.
F7(♭3) Ebsus2 Fsus2 F7(♭3) Ebsus2 F7sus
Flute
Gtr. 2
Gtr. 1
Bridge:
F Cm
Gtr. 1
And the love that I feel
Gtr. 2

Csus2 Cm
Eb
Gm
is so far a - way.
w/Rhy. Fill 1 (Gtr. 1)
Bb
A7sus
I'm a bad dream that I just had
F
A
to - day.
Bb
Csus
Csus2
C
And you shake your head, hmm,
w/Rhy. Fig. 2 (Gtr. 1)
F5
C(4)
Bb
Fsus
Ebsus2
Bb
Flute
and said it's a shame.
Rhy. Fill 1
Gtr. 1
hold
T
A
B
3
5
3
5
6
3

F7(3)
Ebsus2
Fsus
F7(3)
Ebsus2
F7sus
Gtr. 2
Gtr. 1
Verse 3:
F7(3)
Ebsus2
Fsus
Fm9
F7(3)
Ebsus2
Fsus
Fm9
Spin me back down the years and the days
Gtr. 2
Gtr. 1
Rhy. Fig. 3
(end Rhy. Fig. 3)
Gtr. 1
w/Rhy. Fig. 3 (Gtr. 1, 10 times)
F7(3)
Ebsus2
Fsus
Fm9
F7(3)
Ebsus2
Fsus
Fm9
of my youth.

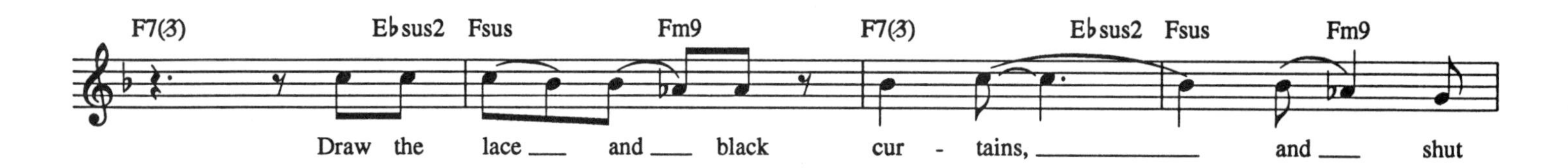

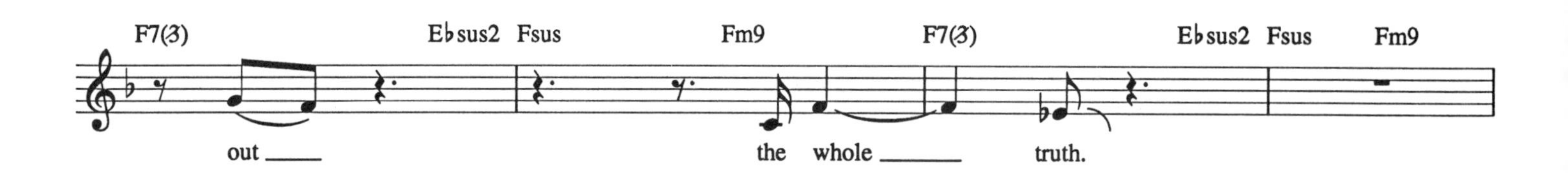

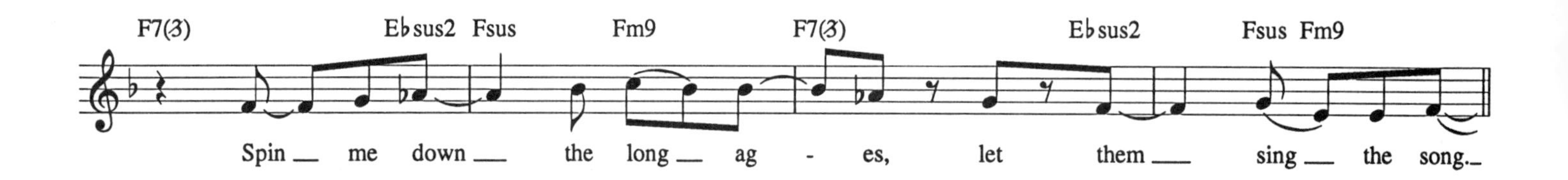

Outro:

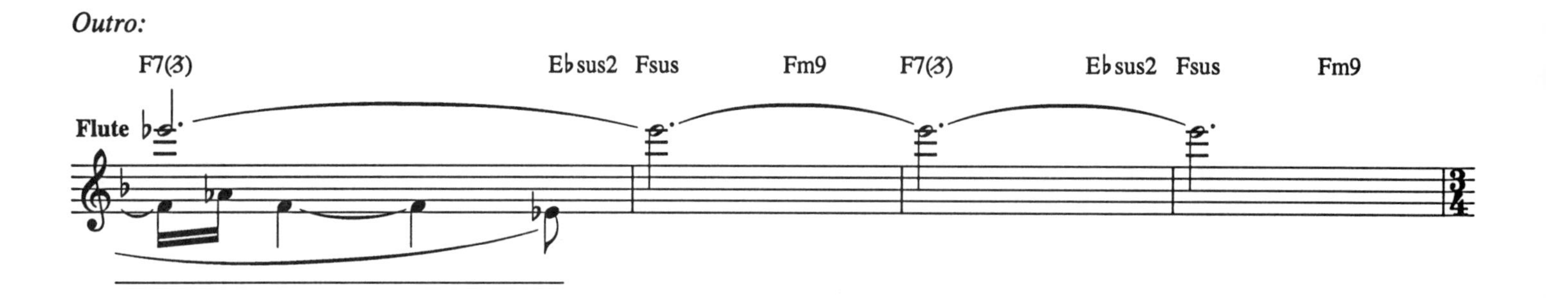

Verse 2:

And the sandcastle virtues are all swept away
In the tidal destruction, the moral melée.
The elastic retreat rings the close of play,
As the last wave uncovers the new-fangled way.
(To Chorus 2:)

Chorus 2:

But your new shoes are worn at the heels.
And your suntan does rapidly peel.
And your wisemen don't know how it feels,
To be thick as a brick.

WITCH'S PROMISE

C
G(4)
Asus2
foo - ool
hold
hold
A5
Asus2
N.C. (A5)
you were kissed by a witch one
hold
hold
night in the woo - ood,
C
G(4)
Asus2
hold-
hold
hold
A5
Asus2
N.C. (A5)
and lat - er in - sis - ted your feel-ings were
hold
hold
hold

C G(4) Asus2 A5 Asus2 C D
true - ue.
hold hold hold
Chorus:
A5 C D A E
1. The witch's prom - ise was com - ing. Be -
2.3. See additional lyrics.
To Coda
(N.C.) A5 Asus2 G D Dsus2 D
liev-ing he lis-tened; while laugh-ing you flew.
hold
N.C. (A)
1.
2.
2. He's

Interlude:
Asus2
Gtr. 1
G6
Gtr. 2 (Acoustic)
mf
Asus2
G6
mf
E
F♯
G
E
G
A
G6
E
F♯
G
E
G
A
G6
Asus2
Keep

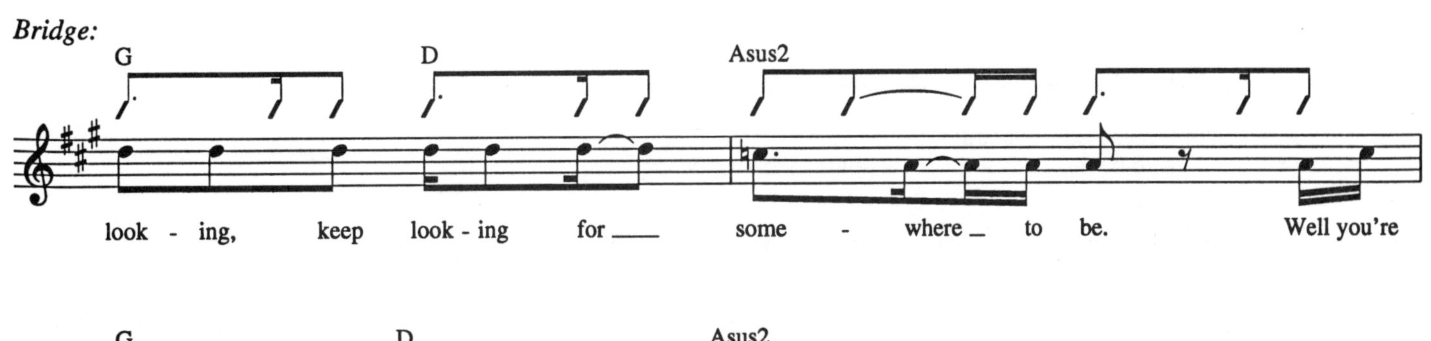

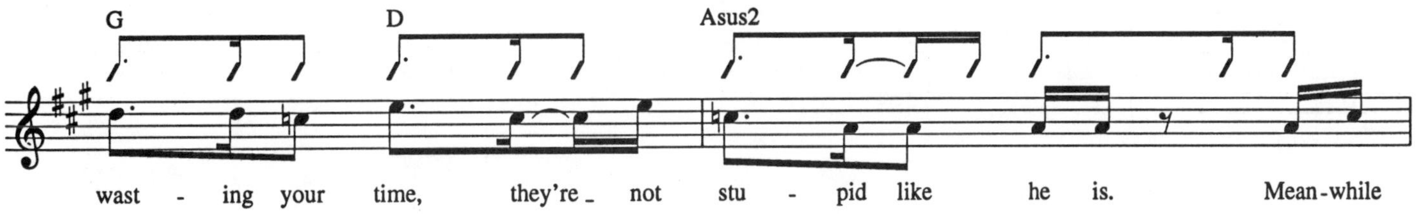

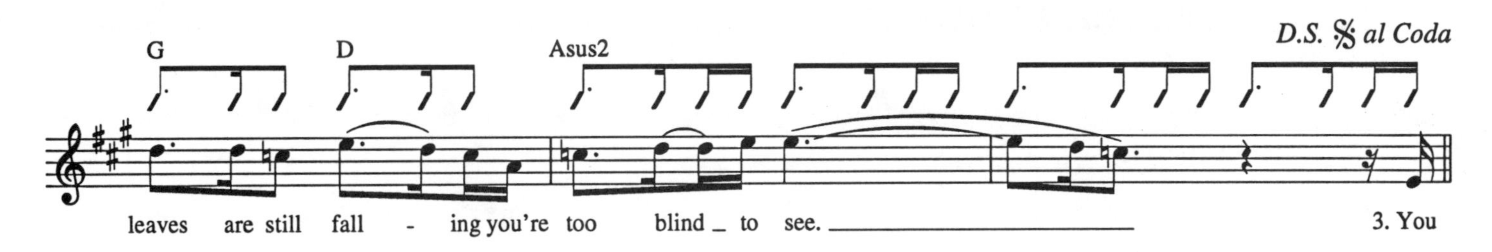

Verse 2:

Leaves falling, red, yellow, brown
All look the same,
And the love you had found lay
Outside in the rain.
Washed clean by the water
But nursing its pain.

Chorus 2:
The witch's promise was coming.
And you're looking elsewhere for your own selfish gain.

(To Interlude:)

Verse 3:

You won't find it easy now,
It's only fair.
He was willing to give to you,
You didn't care.
You're waiting for more,
But you've already had your share.

Chorus 3:
The witch's promise is turning,
So don't you wait up for him,
He's going to be late.

(To Coda)

GUITAR TAB GLOSSARY **

TABLATURE EXPLANATION

READING TABLATURE: Tablature illustrates the six strings of the guitar. Notes and chords are indicated by the placement of fret numbers on a given string(s).

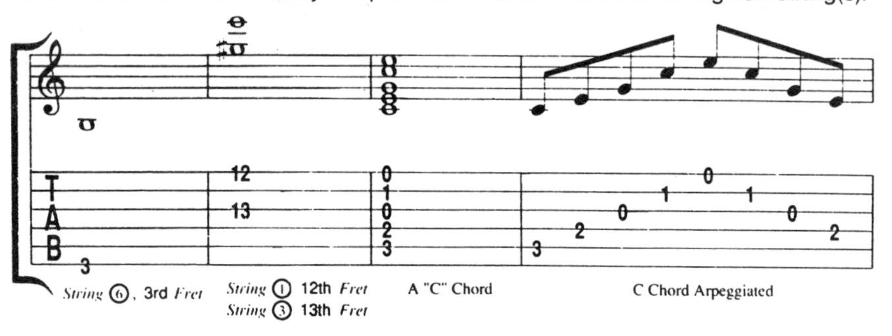

BENDING NOTES

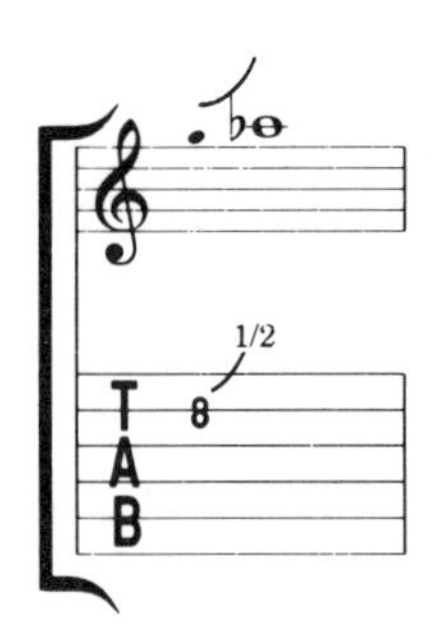

HALF STEP: Play the note and bend string one half step.*

WHOLE STEP: Play the note and bend string one whole step.

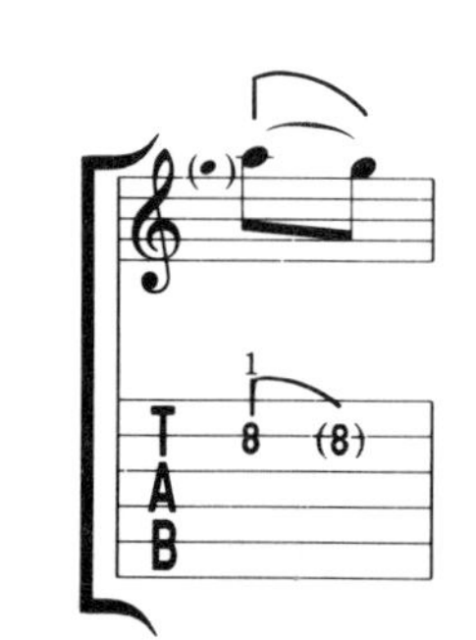

PREBEND AND RELEASE: Bend the string, play it, then release to the original note.

RHYTHM SLASHES

STRUM INDICATIONS: Strum with indicated rhythm.

The chord voicings are found on the first page of the transcription underneath the song title.

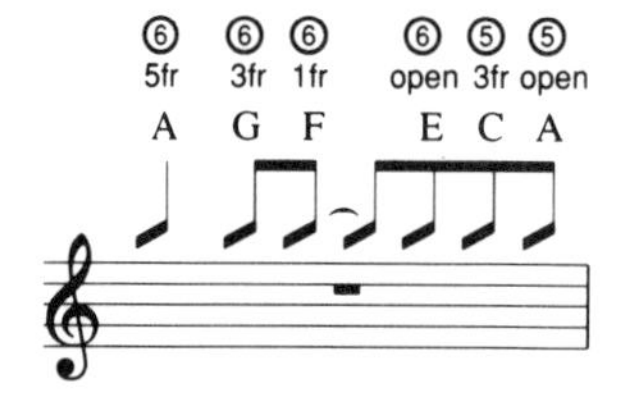

INDICATING SINGLE NOTES USING RHYTHM SLASHES: Very often single notes are incorporated into a rhythm part. The note name is indicated above the rhythm slash with a fret number and a string indication.

*A half step is the smallest interval in Western music; it is equal to one fret. A whole step equals two frets.

**By Kenn Chipkin and Aaron Stang

ARTICULATIONS

HAMMER ON: Play lower note, then "hammer on" to higher note with another finger. Only the first note is attacked.

PULL OFF: Play higher note, then "pull off" to lower note with another finger. Only the first note is attacked.

LEGATO SLIDE: Play note and slide to the following note. (Only first note is attacked).

PALM MUTE: The note or notes are muted by the palm of the pick hand by lightly touching the string(s) near the bridge.

ACCENT: Notes or chords are to be played with added emphasis.

DOWN STROKES AND UPSTROKES: Notes or chords are to be played with either a downstroke (⊓) or upstroke (V) of the pick.